Plano East Historical 40 – 0 Perfect Season
6A Texas Boys STATE Champions

#MAKINGBELIEVERS

Foreword by Mark Lambert

Greg Thomas

Copyright © 2025 by Greg Thomas

All rights reserved.

Author Viewpoints

This is a work of creative non-fiction. The conversations in *#MakingBelievers* all come from the author's recollection, though they are not written to represent word-for-word transcripts. In earnest, the author has retold them in a way that can evoke feelings and memories. No names have been changed, no characters invented, no events fabricated. All incidents and dialogues are real; exact descriptions and dates are true and accurate to the best of this author's memory at the time of the writing.

Foreword

Plano East Senior High Basketball 2023–2024. Forty wins and zero losses. The first undefeated Texas State Champions since 2009 in Class 6A—the highest classification in the state. Multiple players on the All-State, All-Region, All-Area, and All-District teams. Multiple players on Academic All-District teams. Our Head Coach, Matt Wester, won multiple Coach of the Year awards, including State of Texas and National Coach of the Year honors. It sounds like a lot to happen in one season—and it was.

I coached for 32 years before I retired in May of 2023, the season right before the state championship run. We ended that season in the playoffs with a record of 31–5, losing to the eventual State Champion, Lake Highlands. It was their team's closest game of the season. If we had another minute on the clock, I think we would have won that game—and then what? Back-to-back championships, maybe? We'll never know. But what I do know is that in that locker room after the loss, we coaches felt that the next year our team had a legitimate shot at winning a state championship. It would have been the first team title in any sport in the history of Plano East. The boys? They knew they were going to win it. Between the tears and the hugs, every one of those kids promised me they would do whatever it took to go all the way, and I believed them.

Whatever it took ended up being an extension of everything they had done for the past three years. As a coaching staff, we consistently preached several non-negotiable points that we were committed to:

1. We were going to outwork everyone else in the state;
2. We would be accountable for our effort and performance;
3. We were never going to quit during a game.

And the boys bought in wholeheartedly.

In all my years of coaching, I'm not sure I ever had a group work as hard as these guys did day in and day out. While we pushed them to go further, the beauty was that they pushed themselves even more. In the heat of a Texas September, guys who had completed running on the track would go back and run with their teammates who weren't done in order to help them make their time. In the weight room, guys who were finished and exhausted would inspire everyone else to do just five more reps or one more set. If anyone missed a rep or shorted a set, there was going to be someone on the team who called them out and made them do the work. The boys held themselves accountable. We may have laid it out there for them, but they took it beyond our expectations. "Hard work pays off" was Coach Thomas' mantra, and the boys embraced it.

Along with a drive to outwork every opponent came the belief—no, the conviction—that they could win any game. It started with that playoff loss to Lake Highlands. They were convinced that they could have won that second-round playoff game, and they carried that belief all the way to a state championship. They simply refused to lose. They played against teams that had Division I players, teams that were bigger and quicker, and yet they never blinked.

I believe the major reason for their success was pure synergy. A core group of the team had been playing basketball together since the 2nd and 3rd grades. They figured out what their friends could and couldn't do on the floor, and soon it became automatic. There were so many times that someone made a pass they knew shouldn't have been caught—and then suddenly it was a wide-open shot. The team on the floor just knew where everybody else was going to be at all times.

Not only that, but the guys were also as close off the court as they were on it. They did everything together: had dinner together, went to homecoming, went to prom. They were as close a group as I had ever known. It was their long-lasting bond that added the special ingredient to the mix.

They were also a fun group of young men to be around. They were always giving each other hell in the locker room and had developed some pretty good imitations of us coaches. There was a lot of laughing about something ridiculous almost all the time.

Once, we were on the road to Wichita Falls for a tournament, and we stopped at a Whataburger to eat. We went in, ordered, and sat down. As we were waiting for our food, a woman—a complete stranger—came toward us and began chatting with Coach Thomas. Now, Greg will talk to almost anyone, and apparently, he charmed this woman to the point that, just as she was about to leave, she stopped and rubbed his bald head for several seconds.

We were all dumbfounded and giggling, but the boys were rolling on the floor of the restaurant, and as you can imagine, from that day forward, they never let Greg forget about it. Anytime somebody could sneak behind Greg, they would give his head a pretty good rub to gales of laughter.

Which brings me to Greg Thomas. I first met Greg around 1997. He had just started coaching at Plano East, and I was the Varsity Assistant at Wylie High School. Over the next 25 years, as I took different coaching jobs looking for the perfect fit, Greg remained at Plano East. We coached against each other a few times over the years and worked together for the last 20, during which time I had the privilege of coaching Chauncey, his son, for a year. It was probably then that we developed a real feel for what the other brought to the table. I learned what a loyal and unwavering champion he was for all the young men who came through his school. He has a unique perspective on what made this team and these players so special.

But this book is not about Greg or me. It is about this unique group of kids and a magical season. I'm sure all or most coaches can look back and say that they had great teams or players, BUT this team was special. A unicorn, a once-in-a-career type of team. What made them so extraordinary? It was their bond, their accountability to each other, and their love for basketball that helped create one of the best basketball teams in Texas history.

- Mark Lambert

PREFACE

To the novice sports fan, even the mere thought of playing for a state championship is as far-fetched as landing on the moon. Every coach opens his or her tryouts claiming to their athletes, no matter the sport, that they have the makings of a deep playoff or a championship possibility. However, in truth, there are only a handful of teams capable of reaching the pinnacle of high school athletics.

Each championship victory is the same, yet uniquely different in the roads traveled, the collection of players, the biggest atmosphere, and minor upsets, providing a lifetime of memories for everyone involved. From the smallest division of competitors to the largest classification, a packed Alamodome is the destination. Fans and spectators travel for miles to witness roundball's crowning achievement—the raising of the state championship trophy.

When sports columnists illustrate terminologies like magical, unprecedented, or destined to capture the headlines, words like brotherhood and accountability are seldom mentioned. But that's the nuts and bolts—along with playmaking ability and a commitment to the cause—that win games.

Things didn't just happen overnight. The biggest misnomer occurring in the past decade, in and around the great state of Texas, is that high school basketball is a second-tier sport. Most fanatics would've thought that the word was out concerning the drastic change within the circles of the basketball families, but the hardcore gym rats had been quietly witnessing the onslaught of athletic talent moving from the grass to the hardwood, and it's been happening for years.

Rumors spread like wildfire as the signs emerged from the once football-dominant Texas toward a basketball-happy state in the early 2000s. The shift began to manifest itself well before February 14, 2010, celebrating the NBA All-Star weekend in Dallas, Texas. Adding to the mix, the game also featured local standouts Chris Bosh of Dallas Lincoln High/Georgia Tech and Deron Williams, from The Colony High/University of Illinois, along with Kevin Durant, the slim sensation from the University of Texas at Austin—both making their All-Star debut. Then the Dallas Mavericks, with their biggest star Dirk Nowitzki, did the improbable and won the NBA Championship. Anything and everything basketball was full steam ahead.

In most communities, football is still king. However, in the suburbs (5A–6A programs), the rumors circulating in high school football staff rooms were that the number of players leaving the sport for basketball was directly related to the grassroots approach from coaches utilizing the AAU model, including summer tournaments and travel, to excite and sway potential future participants to the gym. When AAU exploded onto the scene, it levied unwanted competition against the football gods for the underdeveloped youth. Along with the possibility of concussions, CTE, and Mothers Against Football demanding rule changes, football drew unsolicited scrutiny abroad and began to lose national popularity. The gridiron was once the most attended and celebrated facility on Friday nights; now the pigskin has a rising opponent and soon could be on the verge of losing twice a week to its roundball brother.

This is only a perception, mind you—a reality which needs no research—but there are those who will attempt to explain why football reigns, and everyone will be the wiser for it.

I am a sports enthusiast, played everything that included a ball in my adolescent years, received scholarship offers to play basketball and football, and my father entertained baseball meetings with a few professional agents but quickly turned down the potential career on the diamond for academics. Education was paramount in the Thomas house. The decision to attend the University of Arkansas gave me the opportunity to pursue both, with a handshake promise that in the spring I could join the Razorbacks baseball program—which didn't happen. I believe in everything football brings to the table, but my first love has always been basketball. And upon looking back, choosing football provided the best challenge at that time and has given me a deeper appreciation for self-motivation, determination, and hard work.

Nevertheless, being in the public service business for nearly half of my life, the work on behalf of our fragile students through modeling and mentorship changed futures. The journey is humbling. Coaching is the escape. It has exceeded every ambition a person could ask for and allowed this ole soul to facilitate life lessons and provide the changes to a much deeper realm than any physical game could produce.

Having witnessed our former students reinvest in themselves and obtain their high school diplomas after previously dropping out of school is overwhelmingly draining. Their life complexities, which were once crippling, are met with positive reinforcement, consistent support, and the requisite tools so the student can gain the necessary confidence and self-worth to complete—better yet, compete—in this crazily challenging world.

This blessing is also, to a great extent, a personal disclosure of hidden emotions. The growth a coach or mentor wants for his students must first be acknowledged from within. Therein lies the problem. Leaders lead—but who and what determines this? Everyone thinks he or she knows what it takes to become a leader. They don't. They only hope or assume. I include myself in this group. It is a sacrifice learned.

I have always been aware of the mountain of responsibility that came with the tremendous opportunity God has provided. As was done for me once upon a time, I now pay it forward to the youth of Plano. A scripture I always share with the players: "To whom much is given, much is expected." – Luke 12:48

The 2023–2024 Plano East basketball team embodies the scripture to the fullest. The expectation for this season was as high as it could possibly have been: 11 seniors, 7 of them returning with 2 years of varsity experience (56 wins), and a deep, competitive desire to make that trip to San Antonio as a team. The opportunity to play for the elusive UIL hardware every team across this great state of Texas has dreamt of.

A commitment to one another—"I Got Your Back, You Got My Back"—an All-In mentality, (Us vs. Them) belief, which each member rehearsed and verbally broadcast aloud as they gazed into one another's eyes while encircled, arm in arm, swaying back and forth after pregame shootaround, prior to walking to the bench for player announcements. A shared unity among brothers brought stares and envy from their opponents and fan base.

When I sat down to write *#MakingBelievers*, I fully expected to bring to life the three-year journeys of these seniors, but what I discovered was that it would be a disservice to narrow this to one year. Twenty years of players, including great stories, from the highest of highs and some of the lowest one wishes to forget. A couple of our low points were so emotional that they demanded tears or required a towel over the face; some worthy of late-night texts and several heated disagreements, but those times led to the most growth in the basketball program. I truly believe we were coaching at our best, and it didn't show up in the win column. Quite often, we do our best when misfortune is present.

If you can stay in the fight, challenge the naysayers, and stand on your beliefs, change will come. Matt Wester did just that. In his six years as the Plano East head coach, the basketball program rebounded and was rebuilt, from a 5–29 first season, and delivered an unprecedented, improbable 40–0—a historical achievement and deservedly to be mentioned as one of the greatest teams to ever lace 'em up in Texas high school basketball.

The Matt Wester message was sent and received. The victory galvanized a hungry community. It awakened the sleeping giant of enthusiasm and belief on the East Side. A first UIL Championship— those same people who once sent emails, had private gatherings, and asked for administrative meetings to remove the staff—were now participating in picture-taking events while shouting and clapping praise. And I don't forget.

Within our small circle at East, the expectation was nothing less than playing in the final scheduled game of the season, Saturday night, March 9th at 8:30 p.m. The opponent wasn't a concern, but if the canasta cards were to follow the state beat writer predictions, Round Rock Stony Point would emerge as a top contender. "That's why you play the game." I eagerly expressed my thoughts to anyone and everyone who asked: "We are the best basketball team in the state of Texas, and if we (EAST) don't win the state championship, it would be all the coaches' fault."

Taking all the pressure and responsibility away from the players, but still giving them accountability and ownership of their practice habits, eating and recovery regimen, along with the mental preparation required to compete at their peak, was on them. Each player earned trust, gained confidence, and believed in the experience from the previous two seasons. The camaraderie and friendships built provided the necessary freedom on the court to be GREAT.

First, the player must believe in the Vision. The Vision was playing for the state championship in San Antonio. Next, the Vision is verbally communicated or spoken into existence. This is done daily in our end-of-practice chant. Afterwards, the Vision is repetitively demonstrated into perfection on the court. When each player understands the Vision, believes the Vision is obtainable, and can demonstrate that Vision, the unthinkable is possible.

The championship was already Plano East's to lose. It was our Reality—we merely had to play the requisite games.

From those crazy weight room sessions to running like tracksters, putting up 500 made shots a day for 3 months—tiresome. It was worth it. Running timed sprints after losing a competitive drill, every day—it was worth it. The endless repetition of sets and plays to perfection—it was worth it.

The team accepted the standard Coach Wester established, and we as the assistant coaches held them accountable—that losing is never acceptable and each player must prepare himself to be the best player he can be today—this became paramount to the team's success.

Our daily breakout: 1-2-3 Family, 4-5-6 State Champs!!!

It is my sincere hope that this inside glimpse of the historical 2023–2024 Plano East State Championship journey provides entertainment, shines a bright vivid light on the enormous sacrifices made by the individual players, their parents and siblings, our coaches' wives, and encourages future basketballers both locally and throughout the great state of Texas to dream big and play harder.

Dedication

To my wife, the amazing Rebecca Lynne, thank you for your unwavering love and support.

To our children: Quiera, Quinae, Da'Ray, Chauncey, Sawyer, Foster, and Jess.

To our grandchildren: Lanayea, Kaiden, Kiyah, Kayleigh, Karter, Kaleb, Kinsley, and Trystn.

Thank you for coming out and joining this journey.

Thank you,

Head Coach Matt Wester

Assistants: Michael Godwin, Chad Evans, Jamie Smith

Coaches' Wives: Micahl, Rebecca, Jessica, Tara

Trainers: Coach Foley and Coach Solis

Head Principal: David Jones

Associate Principals: Ralph Eppler, Shelia Daniels

Principals: Mona Abdelfattah, Stacey Flake, Tracy Lamar, Diana Salazar

Athletic Director/Head Football Coach: Anthony Benedetto

Student Managers: Kaylee Hatcher, Gabby Clinger, KJ Campbell

Student Trainers: Tiffany Phan, Shirley Abrego, Kinsley Slaughter, Elle Madawi

Photographer/Videographer: Leonard Ratliff

Table of Contents

EASTSIDE PRIDE.

Plano East Varsity Basketball
2020-2021

Number	Name	Height	Class
0	Connor Johnson	6'4	Sr
1	Damion Gunnels	6'2	Sr
2	Deuce Hardison	5'11	Sr
3	Isaiah Brewington	5'9	Fr
4	Brandon Hardison	5'11	Jr
5	Jackson Sabey	6'2	Sr
10	Jaydon Nava	6'0	Sr
11	Collis Whitfield	5'10	Sr
12	Jon Tran	6'0	Fr
13	Aiden Hayes	6'5	Jr
14	Muizz Qazi	6'3	Jr
15	Isaiah Hyman	6'4	Sr

Plano East Varsity Basketball
2021 – 2022

Number	Name	Height	Class
0	Morris Williams	6'7	Sr
1	Brandon Hardison	5'10	Sr
2	Akshat Saini	5'10	Jr
3	Isaiah Brewington	5'8	So
4	Jordan Mizell	6'0	So
5	Rachard Angton	5'8	So
10	Xavier Miller	6'1	So
11	Nolan Dickey	6'1	Sr
12	Jon Tran	6'1	So
13	Muizz Qazi	6'4	Sr
14	Aiden Hayes	6'5	Sr
15	Ethan Moss	6'3	So
20	Danny Suliman	6'3	Sr
21	Corey Upkins	6'6	Jr

Plano East Varsity Basketball
2022 – 2023

Number	Name	Height	Class
0	Corey Upkins	6'6	Sr
1	Rachard Angton	5'10	Jr
2	Narit Chotikavanic	6'1	Jr
3	Isaiah Brewington	5'9	Jr
4	Jordan Mizell	6'1	Jr
5	Ethan Moss	6'4	Jr
10	Xavier Miller	6'2	Jr
11	Nate Malone	5'8	Sr
12	Jon Tran	6'2	Jr
13	Ahmad Abualneel	6'4	Jr
14	Seth Romero	6'4	Jr
21	DJ Hall	6'4	So
23	Chima Chineke	6'6	Jr

Plano East Varsity Basketball
2023 – 2024

Number	Name	Height	Class
0	DJ Hall	6'6	Jr
1	Rachard Angton	5'10	Sr
2	Narit Chotikavanic	6'2	Sr
3	Isaiah Brewington	5'9	Sr
4	Jordan Mizell	6'2	Sr
5	Ethan Moss	6'4	Sr
10	Xavier Miller	6'2	Sr
11	Carter Buchanan	6'2	Sr
12	Jon Tran	6'2	Sr
13	Moustafa Abualneel	6'4	So
14	Seth Romero	6'6	Sr
15	Izan Qazi	6'4	Jr
20	Amani Koutsakis	6'2	Sr
23	Chima Chineke	6'6	Sr

My coaching this season, from the bench specifically, would be different. I wanted to challenge myself and appreciate this rare opportunity to coach this group of players. No longer taking down the stats, denoting relevant points, checking off plays, and writing reminders during the game. We (staff) discussed teaching the managers how to keep the book, shooting charts, and defensive categories that needed improvements.

This decision allowed the full appreciation for the flow of the game. Over the years, I seldom celebrated great passes, shots, or dunks; occasionally, the multitasking of taking notes during the game caused me to miss some breathtaking, momentum-changing plays.

I had the best seat in the house. I'm the man sitting next to THE Man, on the front row. And this team had a real likelihood of playing for the 6A state title.

The previous 20 years of keeping stats served their purpose on two fronts. First, I knew or was aware of everything that could happen during the end of a quarter, half, or game. We were prepared for multiple offensive sets for certain players depending on individual performance, and the defensive scenarios were influenced by game scouting reports and subject to change to trapping, switches, or zoning up. Specifics on the opponent's personnel—like knowing the team timeouts, fouls, and who to foul—were required. This allowed me to assist Coach Wester, if he needed, with a spot-on option to choose from.

Second, it kept me focused and out of the way. The players need to hear one voice in the timeouts. The assistants can interject or address pointers and reminders, but time is of the essence and clarity is paramount. I acquired the knowledge of this concept from the readings of *How to Lead When You're Not in Charge* by author Clay Scroggins.

Scroggins' printed work was a welcome challenge and, most intriguingly, insightful.

With that being stated, having the responsibility of doing both—keeping stats and mentally preparing for all the things that could possibly go wrong at the end of a game—is often unsettling and comes with the territory. But the anticipated freedom to only coach is eagerly rewarding.

INTRODUCTION

In 1981, on a September fall morning and located approximately 18 miles north of downtown Dallas, Plano East Senior High opened as the second high school with 560 juniors in the expanding Plano suburban city limits. The school colors, black and Vegas gold, and a panther as the mascot, represent the community just east of Central Expressway, known as Highway 75.

Principal Archie McAfee opened the new high school that fall and proudly steered the course for 25 years. Visionary Dr. Michael McClellan led for 2 years, followed by former East AP Karen McDonald's 7-year stewardship after her second stint with PISD. In 2014, George King assumed the call to guide the Panther Nation and did so for 8 years. David Jones, an East alum and former coach, accepted the Top Cat position.

Since the opening 43 years ago, five principals have directed the student body with dignity and served its community well. Frequently mentioned as one of the nation's largest graduation classes, students have earned the "Best High School in Texas" designation by several magazines, the U.S. Department of Education Blue Ribbon, along with state and national Decathlon Championships. East also offers an International Baccalaureate

1

Program for students throughout Plano and a Health Science Academy. Athletically, East Cheer continues to make respectable showings at state meets. Bowling has obtained 4 State Championships (that I sponsor), and 1 in hockey, both in club/non-curricular activities. East Band, Orchestra, and Choir consistently represent our campus remarkably in state competition.

However, after mentioning the longstanding history and achievements, Plano East was still seeking its first UIL athletic state recognition.

Some people believe that every state championship team is the same. They incorporate a few unique characters, display different strengths or makeups, yet drastically compromise in thought, but in the end, they become winners... and others use descriptive terminology like magical or unprecedented to explain the unexplainable. Each statement is accepted, but neither quite captures the total essence—the special bond developed between the players and coaches, the sacrifices made by everyone involved to accomplish that goal, and the acknowledgment that comes with it.

Not all champions or championships are appreciated, but they should be respected.

"You cannot live a PERFECT day without doing something for someone who will never be able to repay You."

- Coach John Wooden

Chapter I

HWPO

hard work pays off

Hard Work Pays Off!

Hard Work Pays Off!!

HARD WORK PAYS OFF!!!

Every team needs a rally call—something that can energize or give a sense of togetherness, a calling card, so to speak. During a summer session in 2021, "Hard Work" was appropriate because this collection of players knew nothing different. I would randomly use a phrase or shout something to motivate them, to enhance their effort, and to encourage them when they were exhausted. Those grueling 108° days on the track, the brutal weight room sessions with shoulder presses and cleans, squatting like footballers, followed by a demanding shooting regimen, were unexplainable— but they became the foundation each would learn to appreciate.

The players would respond and recite it back after every workout, signifying to one another that this effort would pay off when the opportunity arose. It was sold, and "they ate it like a fat kid eats cake."

Once the buy-in took place, the hard work of running double-digit 100-meter sprints and performing CrossFit exercises had absolutely nothing to do with putting the ball in the net—and everything to do with learning to trust the process. The belief that losing (individually or as a team) at any cost was unacceptable. It wasn't just about verbalizing; it was about the accountability that comes with it. The players seemed to incorporate what each lacked from every basketball competition Coach Wester could muster up. The idea of preparing each practice to be more difficult than any game became common—and a proven endeavor.

Plano East's first basketball head coach, Gary Moseley, and his assistant coach, Rodney Fabre, directed the Panthers to their first state playoffs as the 12-5A district runner-up and a bi-district appearance, with a 26-5 record in the school's second year of existence. East would win the school's first outright district championship in 1987–1988.

Steve Adair assumed the leadership position as head coach in 1989, with assistant Tom Quigley coming from Vines High School, the feeder for Plano Senior. Success followed Adair as he led East to his first district title in 1990–1991—year two, like his predecessor. It was the beginning of three consecutive playoff berths, but the best season in school history, and the only state appearance, came as the district runner-up. The 1993–1994 campaign hangs reverently, center placement, in the Archie McAfee Gymnasium on the campus of Plano East Senior High School, for every spectator to see.

The accomplishments read in bold gold letters on a black canvas: *33-4, State Finalist, Regional Champs, Area Champs, Bi-District Champs.* The appearance in the state championship game vs. Sugar Land Willowridge High propelled the East basketball program's expectations. The seeds were planted.

Adair led the program to another district championship in 1998–1999, two area championships, and his final regional appearance in 1999–2000.

It has been 20 years—fall of 2003 to be exact—when the late Steve Adair, our former head basketball coach and Plano East all-time victory leader (327 wins), approached me about becoming his assistant, along with Doug Bleadorn. Little did anyone know about Coach Adair's battle with cancer, which took his life two years later, but he led the team to back-to-back district titles between stays at MD Anderson in Houston, Texas, in 2003–2004 and 2004–2005. Coach Bleadorn did a masterful job steering the program in Steve's absence during this turbulent time. Doug also was at the helm for a third district title, the school's second-best seasonal record (30-6), and a regional finalist appearance in 2007–2008.

In 2012–2013, East alum and member of the 1993–1994 state finalist team, Jeff Clarkson, took over as head coach. He brought with him Matt Wester as assistant from his Naaman Forest staff, fresh off a state tournament appearance.

Coach Clarkson guided the Panthers to a 30-7 record, a district championship, and a regional appearance in his first season. In 2013–2014, as the district runner-up, East captured a bi-district win, played in an exciting four-team matchup for the final playoff spot in 2014, and went on to win his second district title, become area champions, and reach the regional quarterfinals in 2015–2016.

Six years and counting, Matt has been the mastermind at Plano East. He has weathered several major tsunamis early on. Our scheduling was outmatched, we inherited a difficult, very challenging district, and we suffered some heartbreaking losses in winnable games. To put it mildly, there were grown men shedding tears on Tuesday and Friday nights in the basketball office. One season, East had five wins; the next season, ten.

What's wrong? Where does the blame belong? How can it be fixed? All good questions—but the answers were in the room.

HARD WORK PAYS OFF! HARD WORK PAYS OFF! HARD WORK PAYS OFF!!!!!

It began with the staff challenging each other to become better—to become better men, better role models, better coaches, better communicators, teachers, and mentors. To just be better.

Expectations were better communicated. Standards were set. Accountability was required, and no promises were made. Everything is earned, rewarded, and celebrated. Competition all day, every day. Each drill or station has a winner. Losers have a consequence.

"At the end of the day,

NOBODY

cares about the box score, only about the result".

Chapter II

Up Next

Following the pandemic, in 2021–2022, when everything in the country had shut down, the Eastside community found rejuvenation in our athletic program, especially with basketball. Although the health scare was obviously present, people were tired of being inside, and parents wanted their students outside and active but safe. The fresh air, the sun on the face, and some exercise were exactly what the country and our team needed. Getting the country back to normal was the health advisors' and leadership's top priority, and sporting events could provide the avenues necessary to achieve this goal.

As the travel bans were slowly lifted, protocols and mandates were established with specifications on distancing and seating, at a minimum of six feet apart. Wiping down areas and wearing a mask or facial covering was encouraged.

Like reading from the Alfred Hitchcock book collection, *War of the Worlds*, the UIL provided guidelines for traveling and for seating on buses. Host campuses and athletic facilities were given directives or mandates to strictly enforce. Principals, athletic trainers, and coaches were given expectations that needed to be adhered to prior to the competition. Early on, the extra duties and precautionary activities were tedious, trying, and frustrating, but in order for the games to be played, each did their part.

Gymnasiums that could hold thousands of spectators at any given event were now allowing fewer than a hundred or so into venues. The attendance of family or friends, at best, for basketball or volleyball did not cover the cost of operations. The brilliant idea for streaming games was introduced, and NFHS chose to become the leaders in providing viewership to the family, college coaches, and the fan base. However, the enthusiasm and pure joy of attending a game in person—to scream or holler, sit with classmates, and be outside the domicile—was greatly appreciated.

The team members were six seniors: Aiden Hayes, Muizz Qazi, Brandon Hardison, Morris Williams, Nolan Dickey, and Danny Suliman; two juniors: Cory Upkins and Akshat Saini; and six sophomores: Isaiah Brewington, Jordan Mizell, Rachard Angton, Xavier Miller, Jon Tran, and Ethan Moss.

That old urban saying, "Can't see the forest for the trees," epitomized this collection of players. Each stated they wanted—so, so badly—to be a playoff team, an accomplishment not achieved since 2016, and many did just the opposite. Several had independent workouts versus team-scheduled training, some sporadically, and an equal number of members did not participate at all in summer activities.

A couple of guys returned from injury (Jordan, a leg), a reoccurring injury (Brandon, shoulder), and one new setback (Nolan, knee).

Our front line was one of average high school ball clubs but lacked varsity game experience. Our back court was small, with little experience, but Brandon was eager to learn and competed hard. Missing the offseason and with little summer commitment, the cohesiveness was slow to build.

Everyone could blame the calamity of COVID for its devastating health scare, but every athletic program was practicing how to relearn the winning formulas following a two-year reign of horror and worldwide disruption.

The players, like their student body peers, were eager to get the season going. The fans reciprocated the renewed opportunity to be out and about by packing the East gym in good numbers. Long lines from prepaid ticket sales by QR coding gave assistance to choice seating. Hand sanitizer bottles on every table, in the restrooms, and at the concession stands restored a sense of normalcy and safety for all.

Coach Wester orchestrated a good schedule of games for the Panthers to develop some needed chemistry, to gain early confidence, and achieved his goal by managing a 20–2 mark before the district competition began. East won the Fantasy of Lights Tournament in Wichita Falls, took second place in the Cedar Hill Tournament—falling to state-ranked Frenship High—and won the match grouping in the Allen Tournament.

To be blunt, East was playing remarkably well before the COVID bug hit Morris, our 6'7" senior forward, who was becoming the X factor for the squad. His health and departure turned out to be catastrophic, and as a younger team, we did not adjust and lost 7 of the remaining 11 games.

Although missing the playoffs by one game (third consecutive season to do so) was a bitter pill to swallow, finishing the campaign with a 24–9 record was the next stage in building the basketball program. This sophomore class was well ahead of the learning curve. Competing in District 6-6A—known throughout the state of Texas as one of the most difficult in which to earn a playoff position and nationally recognized as the #1 toughest state tournament to be crowned champion—the East players believe this is within our grasp.

The talent was there. We (as the staff) had to figure out how to utilize the talent, practice in ways to enhance competition, reward those efforts, and incorporate a non-acceptable losing mentality.

Repetition, repetition, repetition. Teach each situation. Make the players do every drill correctly. Make the players accountable for trying to cut corners—don't allow them to cheat at doing the little things. Explain to the players the process and teach them to trust in that process. The *trust the process* philosophy is foreign to the general public. The average fan has very little knowledge or concept of what it truthfully means. Simply put, it means that if one follows the major plan to the letter, the end result will be worthwhile. If provided in small chunks, the players can absorb that belief system and put that action in their memory bank for future recalling.

For the Players

1. Developing a standard is crucial to building chemistry.
2. Hold each accountable.
3. Be competitive (every drill).
4. Commitment to the weight room/conditioning.
5. Demanding toughness.

For the Coaches

1. No jealousy.
2. Don't be the cause of detriment.
3. Bring positiveness to the table.

The change was coming for both the players and the staff. Coaches needed to role-model that change. This accountability began at the top. Each coach came prepared and demonstrated accountability every day and led by example. Instructional discussions and practice plans were specifically scheduled and built in on what skills to practice and teach in order for the players to be better prepared for any and every situation that could win us a game—or conversely, lose us a game.

- Ex: the best defenders in at the end of a game.
- Ex: the best scorers or play to win a game.
- Ex: who to foul, what kind of foul, injuries, turnover-prone players, etc.

For the coaches to teach how to win a game, the coach and staff should be knowledgeable of ways to win and/or not to lose a game. We have been on both sides of this equation. It is maddening if the loss costs you a victory, even if it has been discussed and practiced.

LEARNING HOW TO WIN is first and foremost. Winning must be practiced and should be a priority—a requirement—for every drill or competition that is practiced. The players need to be coachable, trustworthy, and bought in. To buy in, one must be present and doing their part.

We also learned that a summer daily workout plan was necessary and put in place. Open gym at either feeder gym (McMillen/Williams) or East four days a week, with one of the coaches present, and some form of structure applied. Putting up a certain number of shots, form shooting (correctly), and shooting shots at game speed was recommended. It wasn't mandatory, but if the players wanted to get something they never had, they had to do things they had never done.

The hard work was paying off. The vision of that destination—getting to San Antonio—was clearer, yet more was required, and the core wasn't complete.

To reflect and pay respect to all the players and teams that represent the rich Plano East accomplishments, we have relocated the trophy cases and framed pictures to the south wall of the Archie McAfee Gymnasium. The only teams to make the wall must be a district champion or a playoff-winning team. With this year's team, we have a spot for the state champion.

"It's not the Will to win that matters.

Everyone has that.

It's the will to PREPARE to

Win that matters."

- Paul "BEAR" Bryant

Chapter III

February 24, 2023

The month of February was the ending and beginning for the title of this journey, **#MakingBelievers**, the improbable dream season. The retirement of longtime coach and respected friend, Assistant Coach Mark Lambert—who was heavily invested with this group of players—was anticipated and personally difficult to shoulder. Mark was a players' coach and a coaches' coach. His steady demeanor (of which I was very jealous) is what every young coach should strive to achieve: confident, yet even-keeled. Mark wore it well in his 6'4" frame.

With the departure of Lambert, joining Wester and myself would be junior varsity coach Michael Godwin, who was elevated to the varsity as assistant. Michael was more than ready for this opportunity at the next level of promotion after six years. He also had the latest familiarity with players he either coached or coached against during his tenure at Otto Middle School. "D-Rich," my nephew and our assistant coach prior to Lambert, pointed out the young players like Jon and Isaiah as seventh graders to watch when we would visit the feeder school campuses.

Derrick left the Eastside for one season and led Blooming Grove to a postseason appearance but returned to the Eastside as head coach of the girls' basketball program as the COVID epidemic shut down the nation.

Chad Evans was named the new junior varsity coach, coming from John Paul II High School and previously Prince of Peace, serving as president. Chad brings a vast amount of experience and basketball knowledge stemming from his time as an assistant coach, a former head coach, and school administrator.

Coincidentally, this is year twelve for me with Coach Wester—six as varsity assistants and six with him as the head coach—totaling twenty as an assistant on the Panthers' bench. Furthermore, I believe that everything is in place to compete for the most coveted, recognizable sports achievement in high school basketball: a state title.

Rounding out our coaching staff is Coach Inman, junior varsity II.

Player additions to the story were 6'5" sophomore DJ Hall; juniors 6'2" Narit Chotikavanic, 6'6" Seth Romero, and 5'8" Nate Malone. Malone and starting center Corey Upkins were the only seniors.

When one door closes, another door opens. Rachard, after a promising sophomore season and summer workouts, suffered a season-ending leg injury. It was a devastating blow and a lengthy recovery, but his presence at practice and on the bench during games provided inner growth for him as a player and teammate. Rachard traveled with the team, and our staff utilized him as a player-coach—the buffer and vision for his colleagues.

Nate, on the other hand, earned the opportunity to join the team. His tenacity and grit represented what every coach would expect their players' attitude to be—giving his all in every practice and knowing that his name might not ever be called upon when the lights are the brightest. It takes a special player to reconcile this task.

The team was beginning to show signs from a great summer of shooting and conditioning, with each potential varsity player and the returning members attending every open gym, camp, and weight room session. This was a tremendous accomplishment due to not having a regularly scheduled time because of gym availability for two basketball teams, three volleyball programs (including feeder schools McMillen and Williams), cheer practice, and roof renovations.

It has been said, "Three things are vital to success in winning at basketball—fundamentals, conditioning/weight room, and working together as a team."

Today, the players are more skilled and athletically superior, with rules allowing more freedom on the offensive end, but are lacking the fundamentals and the basic knowledge of playing the game. The simple two-handed pass or shot fake aren't practiced. Setting the generic pick-and-roll is seldom executed, and bank shots rim out. Actions like landing on two feet and using your weak hand should be practiced daily, ultimately becoming mastered. Instead, they are considered outdated and mocked—but not in our gym.

This thought is of a loser's mentality, and our staff makes it a priority to coach it out of the guys. Preaching and doing the little, hard things—such as blocking out, fighting for the rebound, and taking a charge—are all selfless, winning plays. These actions are encouraged, celebrated, and rewarded.

Conditioning and weight room work takes heart—or it takes the heart. Fatigue makes cowards of us all. When tired, most lose focus or concentration, fail to perform assignments, and miss opportunities that present themselves. It happens to the best of athletes. East conditioning has very little to do with running and more to do with self-improvement and not giving in to the current challenge at hand. Will this person give his/her all when pushed to the limit? Can he/she function, think, and react when the chips are on the line? Can we trust them? Ultimately, can they trust themselves or their teammates and the coaches?

Coach Wester's weight room workouts stem from cross-training methodology versus powerlifting. All the basic lifts—such as squats, bench press, hang cleans, and incline—are used, but the traditional combinations of set reps are not. Every exercise is timed, with three lifts (arms, legs, and core) for maximum muscle fatigue, followed by a challenge/competition lift for points. Coach preaches that the tougher team will put themselves in a position to win.

The final stage for everyone to embrace was the mental component. The staff had to breathe positiveness into each phase of the preparations. The players were confident, and for team camp at the University of Oklahoma, nothing could have been a better springboard to the upcoming season. The players played with a sense of comfortability and a trust amongst one another that comes after three years of purposely driven expectations, with a "team/me" approach that built a camaraderie which was exhibited from the first day of practice.

Team picture day summed up the players' message in three words: "Back to Business." In conversation with Mr. Roosevelt Joubert—veteran photographer and friend of the program—who was shooting our individual, team, and poster photos, I asked for assistance on the props for this season's theme.

If we could commandeer a classic vehicle, I had an image of the players dressed in business attire staged in front of the gym. Simple and quick, I surmised, but Mr. Joubert took that thought and produced one of our Panthers' best poster shoots. Joubert contacted and obtained permission for the use of a 1972 Cadillac convertible. The fellas changed into their Sunday best while Mr. Joubert photographed the junior varsity squads, then walked outside the gym to put his visionary thoughts on paper.

The dark-colored Cadillac classic, with fourteen players staged inside and around the convertible in business dress, featured the large, monogrammed "Plano East" sprawled across the top of our Archie McAfee gym. Without smiling, the photograph hopefully conveys the appropriate message: "Back to Business."

The shoot took all of 15 minutes.

Now, learning how to win (not lose) is next.

More games are lost than they are won. For example, poor preparation, not understanding situations, one or several players not following a scouting report, or not knowing what a scouting report is or how it can be utilized.

We, at Plano East, provide a detailed scouting report for each varsity player, and I hand-deliver it to the players before every game. The report describes what Coach Wester sees as the keys to victory (reminders) for that specific game. I read this report aloud during our pregame team meeting prior to every game. It is our mental visualization time before Coach Wester's final team words.

The coaching staff at East, along with the assistance of the feeder school coaches, goes over and beyond to give our student-athletes the best chance of being successful on and off the court. Every scenario—from what's a winning play and what isn't, to knowing your individual and team responsibility, and most importantly, understanding situational basketball—is discussed, hashed, rehashed, scheduled into practice, and practiced regularly.

Right out of the gate, a San Antonio tournament at Northside ISD demonstrated signs that East basketball was back on the map and ready to be recognized throughout the state. We easily demonstrated our new physicality and conditioning while handling a field of two state-ranked teams, which included a couple of highly recruited, 5-star players. The Panthers jumped out to a respected 8-0 record.

A mid-morning scheduled contest—11 a.m. to be exact—the following Saturday, November 26th, against Highland Park High, would be our fourth state-ranked opponent in six games. Under legendary Coach David Piehler, earning his 500th victory, the Scots soundly high-flew and dunked their way to defeating us 64-47.

This day, our Panthers did not bring their normal competitive juices, and we were humbled by the Scots. "They were mentally tougher and more physical than we expected this morning," Jordan and Isaiah would state. The confidence that came from the San Antonio tournament wasn't on display. Highland Park jumped out to an early lead and gave us a surprisingly physical beatdown.

After the loss, the twenty-minute bus ride home from Dallas was enough time to drive home a few points into the minds of the guys—that each contest is different and every opponent requires separate preparation. "We didn't adjust today, but we will. Good programs make those adjustments. East is one of those good programs," Wester claimed as the bus parked on the curb of the Plano East campus. "Details matter."

Tuesday's scheduled event, another away game in a hostile environment at Wylie High, provided that needed adjustment. It was the first of two matchups between neighboring towns, with the winner of this hotly contested battle coming down to who could get the stop on the defensive end and which team could handle the execution on offense when it mattered most.

Wylie's big two players versus East's balanced attack. East wins a tightly brewing rivalry, 68-67. The defensive toughness and paying attention to the game plan allowed the five guys in the game at the end to recall schemes and be in the proper position to make a play.

The team was learning how to win.

East travels to Grand Prairie High, and Wester coaches in his sweats. Bus problems caused a minor disruption (a replacement bus was needed) and put the expected arrival time behind schedule.

Another adjustment the team and staff would chalk up to experience. A game that none envisioned to be a difficult battle turned into just that. The GP Gophers knocked down some long-range shots and kept the contest close in the final quarter (equaling 21-21), but East wins.

East 58 – Grand Prairie 49

A Tuesday trip to a possible playoff opponent and former district foe, McKinney Boyd High, was another test of style versus athleticism. We had them in both categories, but players must make plays. DJ, Isaiah, and Jordan scored in double figures, but Narit led the team with 13 points on the evening.

East 70 – McKinney Boyd 62

LEARNING HOW TO WIN

Cedar Hill annually provides a very respected early December tournament and has become a Panther favorite during the last 20 years. It did not disappoint in 2022. East managed to defeat a good Southlake Carroll team in the championship game, 67-53. Among the four-game tour, we defeated Wolfforth Frenship High, Red Oak, and Dallas Madison—all state tournament qualifiers.

A district-opening win over Flower Mound Marcus, 78-37, further gave the Panthers steam as we headed into the Allen Holiday Tournament with the expectations of playing the #1 ranked team in Texas, Lake Highlands High, with the #1 ranked junior in the class of 2024, Tre Johnson, and former Plano East alumnus, Coach Duffield.

However, the first-round matchup vs. Lake Travis and the nationally ranked Hudson Greer was on tap. Greer was a one-man show, and he gave it all he had, but one man is not enough to beat this East squad.

A nine-game winning streak, besting the eight-game start to begin the season. A 17-1 record with the biggest game, not only in North Texas but with the entirety of the basketball universe watching.

In the locker room, several of our players were tentative and mentioned that they needed more time to warm up, wanting to take the court before the Lake Highlands team for stretching. I told the story of former Arkansas Football Coach Lou Holtz and his philosophy on taking the field first.

I asked them a simple question: how many of you have ever attended the circus? A couple or more raised their hands, but not more than five. I proceeded with the tale. After the crowd assembles in the large tent, the Ringmaster, who MCs the ceremony, begins the program by signaling the monkeys, the bearded lady, the fat man, our little people, tightrope walkers, and such to perform tricks, jump through hoops, etc. That's what they call the entertainment of the program.

Then the Ringmaster calls for the elephants, panthers, lions, and tigers with their trainers to perform their acts of death-defying mastery. This is the main attraction—the part the people really came to see.

Coach Holtz's point: we let our opponents go out first; they are the entertainment. We always go out last because we are the main attraction. We come to put on a show. Storytelling and using metaphors can be a great leadership/coaching tool if used appropriately and if it is received with open-mindedness from the guys.

This was my motivational speech of the day—my best attempt to redirect our players while motivating and planting seeds for future reference. They were listening but did not hear me.

Lake Highlands entered this game with a 9-3 record, losing an early contest to former state champions Duncanville High and following with a pair of losses in the Florida tournament against Paul VI (Virginia) and Centennial (California).

LHHS played comfortably, was more aggressive, and made the plays that were needed. We played tight, apprehensive, and did not react to routine situations—as if we were in awe of the moment. Was the stage too big? What was missed? But there is room for growth—lessons to learn and to be taught, for the coaches and players alike.

It's a process. Steps cannot be skipped.

There are levels to learning how to win.

The physical and mental challenges were among the easiest triumphs achieved; however, the process with the emotion was lagging. Understanding that playing with an even keel is the next level of winning—keeping your emotions intact, not becoming too high after a great play or too low following a mistake—wins. Each player had to learn how to let go of the previous play and move on to the next opportunity. This was the final battle and experience they needed to gain.

Following the loss to LHHS, we would take home the third-place trophy by defeating Clear Falls and Wylie High (for the second time in a month) soundly, finishing 4-1 in the Allen tournament and currently 19-2 with a top-15 state ranking. Bigger things were on the horizon for the East basketball team of 2023.

With the student body out, still on Christmas break, Tuesday, January 3, East traveled to Lewisville High School to take on the Fighting Farmers for a district clash. The Panthers controlled all four quarters, securing a 68-57 district win—number two—and setting up for another highly anticipated, North Texas packed gym matchup with crosstown rival Plano Senior High.

When rivals play, no matter the ranking, anything and everything is thrown out the window. A tough, hard-nosed competitive match at its finest, with nothing to lose and everything to gain with one single victory. Two teams with no love lost between them, divided by a highway (Central Expressway). It is literally brother vs. brother. Get your popcorn ready because the excitement was bubbling, and inside the box, heroes can be made.

Plano Senior High, the reigning district champs with 5-star PF Justin McBride and 4-star Tyran Mason, and Head Coach Dean Christian were the front-runners. But we countered with two seniors, Corey Upkins (varsity returner) and Nate Malone; ten juniors, six varsity returners, and four guys with 60 sub-varsity games under their belts; and one emerging sophomore, DJ Hall. All hungry for a run at a district title and hunting for their first playoff appearance—both last accomplished in 2016.

That crazy idiom, "lightning never strikes in the same place twice," or the idea that an unusual event happening again to the same person in the exact same circumstance with the same outcome in the same season is unfathomable.

It did. He did. Not once, but twice. Plano guard Justin Buenaventura hit the game-winning shot to defeat us and became a Plano Senior High hero. As much as Justin was in the right spot at the right time and made the correct play, we didn't do our part. Any one thing—communicating to one another, reciting responsibility, stepping correctly, putting a body on a body—could have changed the outcome.

Plano Senior 60 – Plano East 59

Coaching-wise, and looking back, it is a gut-wrenching, devastating loss that cost us dearly later in the season.

We discussed strategies that can prevent us from such a defeat in the future. Staff could have made situational personnel substitutions, both offensively and defensively, putting our best five guys in during the final minutes of the game—but that's the learning curve.

Three weeks later, the rematch for Friday night was rescheduled to Saturday at 2:00 due to bad weather. The game was touted as the High School Featured Game of the Week, with local television and radio stations requesting credentials. Extra officer presence was arranged in part because of the large crowd expectation, and "The Jungle," the nickname of the student section in the Archie McAfee Gymnasium on the Plano East HS campus, did not disappoint.

The game lived up to its billing, with both teams making runs of 6–8 points throughout the contest. East battled to take a two-point lead after Jordan made a bucket and free throw to complete a three-point play, giving East the lead at 50-49. Coach Christian called a time-out, which Coach Wester followed with a second stoppage to set the strategies for the final seconds. We had fouls to give to stop the game and force them to inbound the ball, using precious clock. The philosophy was to cause enough pressure without allowing the players a good look at the rim or forcing them to use their last time-out.

McBride receives the inbounds toss, avoids contact while taking two dribbles. I immediately screamed, "Foul! Foul!"—the strategy we had practiced and exactly what was discussed during the last time-out seconds earlier. Wester yells, "Foul!" as well, and several spectators are heard bellowing out, "Foul him! Foul!" But McBride makes a cross-court pass to Buenaventura (Justin to Justin), who catches the ball, takes a dribble, pump fakes, and launches a 30-foot prayer. And lightning struck again.

Everyone was learning how to win (not lose). Teaching, reinforcing, and paying attention to doing the little things has to become a priority.

A second loss to our rival is tough, but how we gave up those games was more difficult to swallow because it had been practiced. However, the overall team goal of qualifying for the state playoffs could be earned with victories this week against Plano West, Flower Mound, and Hebron—the third-place team in the district standings. The guys played solidly in their remaining three games, took care of business, and finished the regular season 30-4, co-champions in 6-6A with Plano Senior.

The win against Flower Mound gave the team its 30th victory; only four teams in school history had managed this milestone. But the second-place district placement, due to head-to-head competition with Plano (which we lost), was yet another lesson to learn. If we had managed to hold on and win either contest, the split would have given us the outright title and provided a different path in our playoff matchup.

Individual regular season awards: Co-MVP – Jordan Mizell; NOY – DJ Hall; COY – Matt Wester; 1st Team – Isaiah Brewington,

Jon Tran, Xavier Miller; 2nd Team – Narit Chotikavanic, Corey Upkins.

The playoff scene was set—the boys' basketball program's first trip to the postseason in seven years. With the excitement at an all-time high, the boys' and girls' teams in the playoffs at the same time hadn't happened in several years. While waiting for the 5-6A district to complete their certification, we began our preparations for the bi-district opponent—a familiar foe, McKinney Boyd. The final decision was to determine what neutral site would host the event. Allen High was chosen. The campuses are roughly 6–8 miles apart, about the same travel time for both squads.

Before long, and as the state bracket was close to conclusion, Coach Godwin—who took care of scouting for upcoming opponents—noted that the winner of our matchup with Boyd would likely face the #1 state-ranked Lake Highlands in the second round for the area championship.

No disrespect to the Boyd players, the possible problems they could deploy, or the outstanding season they had, but the background noise around the McAfee gym echoed the desire for revenge after the earlier 17-point defeat at the hands of Lake Highlands in the Allen "In-N-Out" New Year's Tournament.

After a near evenly played first quarter (East up 13-11), the boys took over in the second and third quarters, outscoring Boyd by double digits and taking a commanding lead into the final stanza, 54-31. Cruising to its first playoff victory, East won 69-52. Sophomore DJ Hall led all East scorers with 16; Narit and Xavier had 10 each; Jon, 8; Isaiah and Jordan, 7 apiece. Balanced is the motto.

In order to be a champion, you have to beat the champion.

Before Thursday's practice at Murphy Middle School, our feeder campus, while walking back and forth to the locker room, I noticed the message board in the hallway with the "Quote of the Day" for their Mustang youngsters. It read:

"The hardest part about coaching/teaching is the daily battle to get young people with seemingly unlimited freedoms & choices to buy into stalwart principles like hard work, discipline, consistency, and the incremental gains that develop because of it. It's never about a scholarship or a guarantee; rather, it's always been about coaching/teaching life lessons and providing people with tools for their tool kit." – Unknown

I hurriedly gathered the guys, and we jogged over to the wall for a short period of time to read the quote, but the message did not resonate.

God works in mysterious ways and according to His timetable.

The rematch was set—a doubleheader with Plano East vs. LHHS at 6:00 and Plano vs. Highland Park to follow at 8:00 (or 30 minutes after the conclusion of game one). Location: Moody Coliseum, the 7,000-seat multi-purpose arena on the campus of Southern Methodist University, Dallas, Texas. The opposing coach: former Plano East alum Joe Duffield.

The atmosphere was electric. Big lights. The biggest stage the program had been on in almost seven seasons. The house was packed, as people from all over the Metroplex began making their way into the gym when the doors opened at 5:00.

Learning how to win. We—and I mean everyone—got caught up in the minutia. The family, friends, and fan stuff took off. The players were anxious—not scared—but the environment was that next level, championship level, and these experiences had to be earned.

Lake Highlands jumped out to a first-quarter lead, 22-10. It was more about what they were allowed to do rather than what we didn't do. Sure, we missed shots and assignments, but it was like we were tired—slow to recognize the speed of the game and the basketball do's and don'ts. The second quarter didn't fare much better; we managed just 21 first-half points and gave up 36.

Halftime adjustments were made; the guys took on the challenge and dug deeper than they had ever done for one another. The third quarter became a battle, fought to a 19-18 even stanza; however, the momentum had shifted to the East. Coach Wester chose to foul—putting the responsibility on the Lake Highlands players to make their foul shots to put the game away. We, on the other hand, began to make our shots and applied pressure on their guards, with an emphasis to foul them harder (mentally, physically, and psychologically challenging their resolve). This appeared to be effective.

The Lake Highlands players missed several one-and-one foul attempts, and we scored on all three possessions—a nine-point swing. Timeout called by Coach Duffield. Traded buckets, then a technical foul and another four-point swing. The second stoppage by Duffield. East down five with just under two minutes remaining.

Moody was near capacity now, as fans from all four programs and others from the Metroplex were intensely watching—heavily invested in the competition taking place on the floor.

They just happened to make one more play than East did: made the free throw, bounced the pass around the bucket, dove for the loose ball. It was converted, and Lake Highlands survived with a 66-63 area championship win.

The game was epic, and it propelled both programs. In Pat Riley's book, *The Winner Within*, Coach explores how to navigate setbacks, failures, and unexpected obstacles. Is this our stumbling block, or is it a stepping stone?

The victory that didn't take place on the floor did, however, take root in the locker room afterwards. In between the tears and hugs, there wasn't a dry eye. With the "I'm sorry" and "I will hold you accountable if you do the same for me," the challenges by the players to the program and to each other became the springboard to their greatness. That commitment to excellence is something I have never witnessed in my 20 years of coaching.

Learning how to win is real. It takes everyone involved.

The evening of February 24, 2023, serves two purposes—the ending of a great season and the beginning of history in the making with this junior group.

How To OVERCOME Failures

1. Short Memory
2. Calm Down
3. The Next Play Is Mine
4. Don't Be Afraid to Fail

However, our approach needs to be pragmatic. There is no such thing as failure, but there is defeat. Defeat isn't failure—it is a missed opportunity. But if we want to reach that next level, everyone needs to be willing to learn.

Learning how to win also means seeking what past champions did on their quest and applying it if it fits our team philosophy and style of play.

Examples: 5A Boys State Tournament in Austin, Texas, on the campus of the University of Texas.

2006 Plano Senior High Boys State Champs.

Under Head Coach Tom Inman and Assistant Phil Parlin, the Wildcats were tough, mean, and introduced a strong inside game presence. Their approach reflected the head coach, who was a South Chicago native and utilized physicality and intimidation with Joseph Fulse, 6'7" F/C (Tyler/Marquette); Eric Zastorpil, 6'8" F/C (Army); Lawrence Mann Jr., 6'5" F (Howard); and 6'4" G, Landon Skinner. Plano had skill players, but 5'10" guard Josh Roberson—named Mr. Basketball in Texas in 2007 following his senior year and a Texas Tech recruit—controlled the tempo.

Plano reached the state finals as the #3 ranked club with a 27-7 record. Along the way, they defeated two state-ranked teams, Duncanville and Berkner. Their opponent was Humble Kingwood, a suburb of Houston, ranked #4 at 36-5 and boasting a talented squad led by G Nic Wise and 6'7" F Mike Singletary.

Humble Kingwood built a commanding lead in the 3rd period, topping off at ten, before Plano mounted four consecutive stops—stop after stop after stop—and Roberson hit a three, followed by another three, and a third triple to force overtime. Wise, however, was equally up to the task, matching Roberson bucket for bucket down the stretch, and he displayed championship form on his final shot. But the ball circled the basket—three to four full rotations—before the basketball gods made their decision, rimming out.

The Frank Erwin Center, "The Drum," was energetic all day, with Dallas Roosevelt winning the 3A, Ft. Worth Dunbar under Coach Hughes taking the 4A, and Plano Senior finishing the tournament with the most exciting ending of a championship game at that time—the first Collin County boys' team to capture a basketball state championship.

2015 Plano West Senior High Boys 6-6A State Championship.

Under Head Coach Anthony Morgan, Assistants Nathan Leraas and my nephew Derrick "D-Rich" Richardson, Plano West had a star-studded roster including Ohio State commit Mickey Mitchell, 6'8" G/F; 6'10" C Tyler Davis and 6'7" G/F DJ Hogg, both Texas A&M signees; 6'3" UCLA football commit Soso Jamabo; 6'8" PF Emeka Obukwelu, a UT-Tyler commit; and sophomore G Chris Giles.

West entered the title game on a 19-game winning streak, with a 33-2 record, ranked #1 in the state. The only blemishes were an early loss to Montverde Academy, a private school powerhouse in a Florida tournament, and a late December defeat to Arkansas basketball power Little Rock Parkview in the championship game of the 58th Annual Whataburger Tournament in Birdville, at W.G. Thomas Coliseum.

Houston Clear Lake came to the challenge with an outstanding record of 35-2, losing only to Fort Bend Elkins and Clear Creek. An overtime rubber match with Clear Creek in the Regional Quarterfinals secured a state tournament appearance for Clear Lake. They defeated San Antonio suburb Schertz Clemens 78-69 in the semi-finals.

In 2015, the University Interscholastic League moved the historic boys' and girls' state tournament from the University of Texas at Austin, 70 miles south, to the Alamodome in San Antonio. The reasoning and solution behind the UIL's decision to change the location came down to availability, affordability for the participants, the overflow of crowding, and finding a better fit for both the boys' and girls' tournaments and the city.

The game between Clear Lake and Plano West added more excitement to the change of venue in its first year hosting the basketball festivities, with the vibrant San Antonio atmosphere.

The Falcons and Wolves battled in an entertaining back-and-forth clash from beginning to end. Late in the 4th quarter, DJ Hogg made two game-changing plays for Plano West, beginning with taking a charge with 11 seconds left, ending Clear Lake's potential of getting a late lead from the charity stripe. On the following inbounds, Hogg received the ball at midcourt, hustled two dribbles, and pulled up for an 18-foot rainbow that hit nothing but the bottom of the net.

Pandemonium... Plano West 56 – Clear Lake 54.

Dog pile at center court in the inaugural Alamodome 6A state championship final game of the evening. Players, coaches, cheerleaders—everyone jumping on and around DJ. What a scene. I even sat up on the edge of my seat, pulling out my phone and starting to text Morgan and D-Rich my congratulations on bringing home the chip.

Instantaneously, as I finished my text to the Plano West coaching staff, anxiety and motivation overwhelmed me at 10:15 p.m. How can we get Plano East over the hump? What can I do better? Teach better? Inspire them to work harder? Questions, but no answers given.

The thoughts began to flood my mind—"Hating every beautiful moment of the Plano Senior and Plano West state championship wins" puts everything into perspective for me. The competitive juices were getting the better of me.

We would start next week. With my own son, Chauncey, Chris Parker, and Devin Gifford, this junior class was close to becoming a contender for a state championship bid next season. But everything would begin with our offseason preparation and buy-in.

Turn off the television and get some rest. I/we have an entire week to prepare since Plano ISD is on spring break.

That was March 14, 2015.

Hard Work, Pays Off

Expectations

Attitude

Recovery

Toughness

Chapter IV

Final Pieces (The Team)

"It has been a very, very long time since I've been this excited about an upcoming season, and I shared my exuberance with everyone who crossed my path. I often claimed that if the Panthers did not win the state championship, the blame should be placed squarely at the feet of the coaching staff." These were not only my thoughts but those of Assistant Coach Michael Godwin as well.

The East basketball program, during the off-season, had seen its fair share of returning players who wholeheartedly invested in getting physically and mentally stronger, but nothing like the spring that had just passed. Player to player, they challenged one another, and the test results reflected it. Looking bigger in the chest, with cut and defined arms, coupled with a new track regimen combining sprint and distance conditioning, well-oiled machines were in development. Their hard work was showing early signs of paying off.

Next season, when we enter each and every gym, my vision is to turn every single head and draw both eyes, signifying awe and excitement as Plano East walks through the doors. Embodying that SWAG, yet maintaining a modest confidence as the home crowd takes its first glance at the best team in the state of Texas. All Eyes on Us.

Our coaching staff honestly believed this squad had all the ingredients necessary to become a threat. The talent was seasoned, after winning 25 and 31 games, respectively, as sophomores and juniors.

With heightened expectations outside the building, no less were the same beliefs held in the office or the locker room. Expectation breeds pressure. Self-perceived pressure is the worst, and pressure can burst a pipe, but the core had been training for this opportunity. The phrase often used is "iron sharpens iron."

The Mount Everest of expectations was planted as a seed the night of the Lake Highland loss, with the individual promise to outwork every team on the schedule and to represent the Eastside community by playing in the final game of the basketball season, Saturday night in San Antonio, 2024. I gave a daily reminder— HARD Work Pays Off—at the end of every workout and practice.

The hard work pays off mantra was purposely added as a rallying cry among the members, signifying their sacrifice made that day. The chant later became a part of the team circle following the pregame warmup prior to competition. A verbal recitation while gazing into the eyes of a teammate before a contest is hypnotic.

My lovely wife, Rebecca Lynne, cut out the saying in large black and gold letters, and the words were taped above the door as a visual reminder where the coaches and players could boldly see and read them when exiting the locker room.

Even with a senior-laden team, the return to basics and fundamentals needed to be retrained. Not only were they quite possibly the best skill-set group, they were also academically the smartest collection of players to suit up for East in my 20 years of coaching. With that being stated, no steps were skipped.

The standard was in place. Fundamentally, the little things became huge: tucking in your jersey, having shoes tied before entering the gym, wearing the school-color gear. Everything was retaught, practiced vigorously, and praised daily. Individually, they were good, but collectively, they could be great. Getting each player to make the sacrifices necessary to achieve greatness was the challenge.

Coach Wester designs every practice around three basic principles: Competition, Skill Work, and Conditioning. Every drill has a winner and a loser. The losers have some form of consequence, like towel pushes, dummy jumps, or timed running sprints. This reinforces responsibility and effort. It also aids in conditioning. Don't lose. Skill work—from ball handling to shooting drills like racing to 50 makes off the glass, from the midrange, off the wing, or shooting behind the arc—are used for both competition and skill and reinforce muscle memory. Finally, Conditioning speaks for itself. It separates the pretenders from the contenders.

Beginning with competition, iron sharpens iron. The guys thrived on pushing one another. There could be any of five or six players who could win the sprints after suffering through competition. Eleven-second down-and-back—Rachard or Xavier, the quickest, easily should win, but Jordan and Narit challenged every single time. Our longer sprints, like down-and-back in 22 seconds and the 8 in 30, required more consistency and heart. The members were primed. Instead of becoming arduous, their focus looked beyond the moment at hand toward the long-range goal of playing in early March in San Antonio.

Our biggest component of competition is the daily division of the members into a black and gold group, and every shooting drill, one-on-one defensive station, or team challenge has a winner and a loser. The winner receives a point, and the loser has a consequence: a towel push, a timed running sprint, dummy jumps, or 50-pound kettlebell swings. A simple reminder that we won't allow losing to be a part of Eastside DNA.

This is Coach Wester's team character-building philosophy.

Skill work—shooting—became the reward from the competitive demands. Every form of shooting drill was explored: (Duke Shooting) 30-second timed shots, rotating from the five spots outside the arc to (Celtic) 3:00 minute drills, and earning the License to Shoot continued the motivation to improve.

The more conditioned team will function better in crucial situations and at the end of games. "Fatigue makes cowards of us all," attributed to former Green Bay football coach Vince Lombardi, emphasized the importance of physical and mental conditioning. Tiredness can make players more susceptible to negative thinking and poor decisions.

Good players practice well every day individually, and great players practice greatly. We have greatness under development. Giving them the opportunity to become great as a team, providing total focus to do what has not been accomplished within the Plano East athletic community, is within reach.

The intensity of the daily grind at practice was interesting, exciting, and energetic. The team genuinely loved being around each other, whether on the court, in the weight room, on the track, at functions, or eating dinner. They wanted to be successful for their brother.

Teach – Practice – Encouragement was enjoyable among the coaches. Hard coaching followed with individual and collective praise between the players during and after court sessions fostered a trusted union that should last a lifetime.

Every season, as a returning player, the opportunity to make personal changes within the locker room is allowed, if available. For example, a player can ask for a new uniform number or a locker move. Following his being named Newcomer of the Year, now a junior, DJ changed his jersey from #21 to #0, like Corey and Morris had done the previous two seasons. DJ played about half the time in every game as a sophomore, but he has big-time dreams and big shoes to fill.

Rachard, a 5'10" senior guard, missed his entire junior season due to a torn ACL, and I was excited to see his return to action. He became like a player-coach while in rehab, and it should benefit everyone when he figures out his role. He will be the missing ingredient for the team this season. A three-year varsity participant.

Narit, the jack of all trades, is the "I'm going to prove you wrong" guy. The best all-around guy on the team. He can score it, defend it, and is not afraid to accept every challenge given. Second-year varsity letterman. All-District last season.

Isaiah, the best point guard in the state. Team captain. Stable, dependable, and tough as nails. A four-year varsity participant. All-District last season.

Jordan, Team Captain, and at 6'2" the best rebounding guard in the nation and the most consistent player on the team. He possesses the quickest bounce to date and comes to work every single day with one thing on his mind: getting that rebound. A three-year varsity letterman. All-District, Co-MVP.

Ethan, 3-point specialist, our "Downtown Freddie Brown." A 6'5" wing who can shoot the rock. A three-year varsity player.

Xavier, the emotional leader with next-level athleticism and moves. A 6'2" guard with hops who can defend. A three-year varsity letterman. All-District last season.

Jon, with the most dedicated shooting ethic I have ever witnessed. Jon made 9 threes as a freshman and sophomore, then sunk 80+ three-pointers as a junior. A four-year varsity participant. All-District last season.

Seth, 6'6" C/F, the most selfless teammate. Second-year returner.

Izan, 6'4" W, first-year player and the most athletic member of the team.

Chima, C/F, DE on the football team, the crowd favorite, and knows his role. All-District in football last season.

After the footballers' tryout, the players added to the varsity from the junior varsity lockers were 6'2" senior guards, Carter Buchanan and Amanni Koutsakis, and 6'5" sophomore, Moustafa Abualneel.

Carter's father, Brett, a member of the '94 Plano East Finals Runner-Up squad, was a guest speaker to the team last season prior to the playoffs. Amanni's father, "J Cruz," would provide next-level excitement to the Jungle with his MCing and arranging of music entertainment during home games.

The team poster is the last challenging obligation the seniors have total input on. During seventh period, Ethan, Rachard, and Jon were given the task of participating in the theme development. Coach Godwin and I brainstormed for a couple of weeks trying to wrap our heads around a common thought, but nothing seemed to make sense or fit the players' personality.

We considered the background of the Alamodome or even a silhouette with a map from the area regional site to San Antonio. Adding the mileage from our Plano East gymnasium to the Alamodome—295 miles—but my Mapsco dialed up the incorrect distance, and that idea dropped. The players and coaches had a good laugh at this mishap. We entertained a train theme as the poster, and I visited the surrounding cities of Garland, Sachse, and Wylie for possible photo shots. Downtown Plano had a railroad red caboose, but we were looking for an engine, not the end of a train. "What kind of message would that send?"

After multiple conversations with Ethan, Rachard, and Jon, three of the seniors with their sixth period off, a movie theme took off. The guys quickly theorized using the theater, used the dry erase board to draw up a background, and discussed getting popcorn containers and 3D glasses as props, basketball, and wearing the new gold jerseys. Wester walked in and said jokingly, "Get your popcorn ready," and the fellas laughed it off. Then he said, "Punch Your Ticket." Right then and there, our poster was formed.

Time was running out, and Coach Wester did not want to relinquish too much practice time toward this project; however, he gave Godwin and me a 30-minute window to get everything completed. I had previously spoken with the East theater teacher, Mr. Grunkowski, about basketball using the auditorium for a photo shoot, and permission was granted. Leonard, an East graduate and former basketball player, now a photographer and documentarian, took 15–20 photos of the players in the auditorium, and we were back on the court within the allotted time frame Coach Wester authorized.

Last year's poster, 2022–2023, photographed by Mr. Joubert, with the players dressed in suits alongside a convertible Cadillac staged outside the gym, was classy and to the point: 'Back to Business.' And a 31–5 season ensued. 2023–2024 is a bolder statement—come out and watch the greatest show on the hardwood. 'Punch Your Ticket' left little doubt about the high expectations for this season.

#MakingBelievers.

The FINAL PIECES were in place.

"The best thing you can do for a person is to inspire them. That's the best currency you can offer: INSPIRATION"

- Nipsey Hustle, RIP

Chapter V

Early Expectations

By late July, though, the excitement surrounding the Plano East athletic departments was at an all-time high. Both football and volleyball had playoff goals, but the basketball program's desired result was a bit more ambitious. The players were gung-ho about improving on last season's 31–5 record, but the simple achievement of qualifying for the playoffs was slightly lower than the big-picture goal of playing on that final day of high school championships in the Alamodome… and that visual was forming.

Head Coach/Athletic Director, Tony Benedetto, provided t-shirts to all the Eastside coaching staff with the new Panther emblem, the new color scheme, and the words "All In." A clear message of unity for every team and staff was sent and totally expected.

A major part of the "All In" concept was the implementation of Cole Carter's strength and conditioning program. Coach Wester, over the years, had changed the basketball workout program to fit the cross-training, sport-specific model, and the transformation was instantaneously visible. Our players' physiques, arms, and shoulders were bigger and more defined, and the weight lost by DJ was gained by Jordan, Xavier, and Isaiah. Their physical strength, earned in the weight room, oozed into the mental confidence the guys were demonstrating on the court.

The overall team strength, through measurements, increased 45–50%, which meant that every player tested out stronger than when they began. Whether in reps or max, each individual player was statistically stronger by the numbers. They looked the part of a weight-trained ball club with bigger, defined arms and shoulders and played more confidently.

Along with the conditioning, our team stamina needed to increase. Stamina allows individual players to continue their play in longer stints of action without becoming fatigued. "Fatigue makes cowards of us all," the truest statement for all athletic competitions. When a player is tired, he or she stops functioning mentally or physically, and plays are missed as a result.

Stamina is always the first to go. The ability to make the normal, fundamental play when tired or stressed is a learned action and must be practiced, practiced, practiced. The best ability is availability.

Another measurement utilized was the physical training test offered by Staff Sergeant Terrence T. Andrews, the U.S. Army recruiter on the East campus. Staff Sergeant routinely stopped by the gym when on campus recruiting possible students for enlistment and showed interest in the basketball program. He discussed with Coach Wester a field test and allowed the players to perform the same physical test given to all recruits. It was a provocative invitation, with timed stations, pulling or dragging weighted objects, and bodily activities, but the guys passed with flying colors.

The fall sports activities—football 3–1, volleyball 22–10 before district play, and cross country placing or winning meets early— were all off to great starts, and the campus was buzzing, as witnessed during the first student pep rally of the year. Basketball was one month away, but the showings at practice games and in pre-season shootouts provided observable signs of promise, and the enthusiasm became evident as t-shirt sales and memorabilia sold out, visibly spotted throughout the congregation during the other sporting events.

Another clear, distinguishable indication of high expectations is when your opponent opts out of playing scheduled games. These things occur from time to time, for whatever reason or rationale, but when East wasn't as potent, we NEVER asked to be removed from a scheduled game or tournament. However, our program was once declined from tournaments because of poor play—but not currently.

Coach Wester now had the opportunity to schedule the best state-ranked teams, including invitations into the best before/after-Christmas holiday tournaments, and play in front of the most hostile high school crowds within the Metroplex.

The schedule reads:

First game of the season vs. Allen High, a former district rival and state-ranked, in the Cowtown Tip-Off at North Crowley High. Teams separated by 6.5 miles will travel 65 miles to battle. Game #2 vs. Highland Park, at home, but a return matchup from last season's schedule and a Scots victory.

A late invite to Duncanville's Thanksgiving Hoopfest was, to the East players, a dream come true. Every young player in North Texas who's a basketball enthusiast wants to be a participant or attend the famous holiday showcase featuring some of the nation's best individuals and top-ranked teams. East will face Springdale High, an Arkansas finalist in their state tournament. A good performance offers the team a golden opportunity to send a loud message to the basketball coaches around the state of Texas.

Visits to Waxahachie and Rockwall, with two four/five-star players and state rankings, will prepare the squad for the possible hostile environments in the future.

East received and accepted an invitation to the Mavs Classic, a local tournament in Frisco, Texas. The chance to play C.E. King, 6A out of District 21, with Atascocita and Beaumont United, added an early match with district foe Hebron or 5A state-ranked Mount Pleasant. The challenge to participate in the CBI, formerly known as the Whataburger, meant leaving the Allen Invitational Tournament. The probability of facing Stony Point, the #1 ranked team in the TABC/UIL, is excitingly expected.

After two years of conversations and failed attempts, Fayetteville High Head Coach and longtime friend, Brad Stamps, invited us to play in their Fayetteville High Hoopin' on the Hill tournament in Fayetteville, Arkansas. This tournament provides the challenge of playing with a shot clock, experiencing different coaching styles, and allowing the team travel growth and experience.

All in all, the 2023–2024 schedule has us playing 25 games on the road with the real possibility of playing 7 additional games, if earned, in the final game of the season. That could be 32 of 40 road appearances. The result of going 31–5 last season, returning 7 seniors with 3 years of varsity playing experience and 11 total, has its perks and its drawbacks. Expectations are higher than ever.

The first weekend in June, the group traveled to a team camp on the Texas State campus in San Marcos, Texas. Something special was developing, and the collective team energy—an inspiring evolution—was on display. Playing unselfishly, passing the ball, moving and screening, communicating on defense, and showing excitement for one another demonstrated that oneness every successful championship team exhibits. Most importantly, team accountability was emerging and becoming apparent. The team finished 3–0, but more importantly, they were showing basketball maturity.

In the event promoting our players, I asked Texas State Associate Head Coach, Bennie Seltzer, if we could have a tour of the basketball facilities, and he graciously obliged. Head Coach Terrence "TJ" Johnson closed out the team camp and joined the tour in the locker room. Both men greeted all the players one by one, but showed little interest in the seniors. However, Coach Seltzer took a liking to DJ.

Later in June, East would be featured in the Texas Association of Basketball Coaches Showcase (TABC) against Beaumont United, San Antonio Brennan High, and Round Rock Stony Point High—three of the top-ranked teams in 6A, the largest classification in the state. Beaumont, a perennial power, was fresh off last year's state appearance. Both Brennan and Stony Point returned veteran players from a deep run in the playoffs, as did East.

We at East believed that the matchups would be an indicator of how the players had grown and should put the program on the map.

To no great surprise, it was a coming-out party individually for DJ, Narit, Isaiah, and Rachard. Each played consistent, steady ball, while Jon, Ethan, and Jordan did the dirty work and made the routine, timely buckets. East defeated Brennan by 30 and Stony Point by 25, but lost to United in the final minute of the game. I commented to Coach Green and his wife in the walkway, "We will see you in San Antonio."

The tone was set, and the basketball pundits took notice.

SELF – DISCIPLINE

begins with the mastery of your thoughts. If you don't control what you think, you can't control what you do-

- Napoleon Hill

Chapter VI

Believing the Hype

It's almost embarrassing to admit, but it's true: there hasn't been a day in my coaching life when I haven't spent some time thinking about winning a state championship and what it would mean to the community of East Plano. That accomplishment is the one thing which sets our sporting families apart from the Plano and Plano West ranks, each with basketball and soccer (boys/girls), and Plano with seven in football.

Now we, East, are vying for that recognition—that elusive first in school history—a State Championship. Thirty years back, this season, Coach Steve Adair and Assistant Coach Tom Quigley led the Panthers to our only state tournament appearance before falling to Sugar Land Willowridge in the finals, 44–50.

The biggest challenge to Coach Wester was making a schedule that could bring forth the most growth for the team (specifically Jordan, DJ, Jon) while providing hostile environments and playing against top-rated teams/players in the Metroplex. Often, when teams return big-time players or receive statewide recognition, coaches ask off the schedule or won't honor last year's game. That was the case for our ball club.

Coach Wester managed to put together a 31-away-game schedule: three tournaments—Dallas Mavs Classic in Frisco, Hoopin' on the Hill in Fayetteville, Arkansas, and the CBI, formerly the Whataburger, in Mansfield. Only nine home games total: Highland Park and Rowlett that first week and seven district opponents to visit the Jungle this season. Two shootouts: one in Wichita Falls vs. Oklahoma's top high school programs, and the South Dallas Shootout vs. 5A State Champions, Lancaster High, and host 5A contender, the Carter High Cowboys.

Allen High in the Cowtown Tip-Off at North Crowley High for the season opener, with road games at Rockwall, Waxahachie, and McKinney Boyd—all coming from playoff appearances and with 4–5 star-ranked players.

The schedule reflected the confidence of the staff—or better yet, the work ethic and belief of the players, their goal this year. The hype is real. The process is even more real. The journey is forthcoming.

In-house, though, within the locker room, everyone was aware of the rare possibility of being a part of something far bigger than individual goals. A daily quest of understanding the moment, not taking anything for granted, striving to be the best player I can be today, and becoming a better teammate was a foundational piece to the puzzle.

Our staff preparation was to make practice harder than the games. By placing pressure on the guys, or making them comfortable in uncomfortable scenarios, with repetitions— repetition until perfection was complete. With emphasis on doing the little things correctly every time, executing the finer points can lead to game-winning plays. Game-winning plays like deflections, diving on the floor for loose balls, and taking charges are momentum-changing actions we consider paramount to becoming a successful program.

The most substantial advantage for the Panther basketball program is in the scouting department, headed by Varsity Assistant Coach Michael Godwin. Coach Godwin assigns and coordinates the scouting by utilizing the middle and high school basketball coaches to watch in person or on video, every opponent. The information obtained is put into a one-page report giving their personnel, height, weight, tendencies, strengths and weaknesses, with sets or plays, etc.

The staff and team members will watch video, read over the personnel, and discuss the report in walk-throughs, on the bus ride or classroom, and in the locker room during pregame preparations.

I absolutely believe that our team is the most prepared and best-prepared ball club in the state, and that's tremendously due to Coach Godwin's expertise and insight.

Everything is now coming together:

After a stellar showing in the Great American Shootout (GASO) in early September against top-rated Duncanville and North Crowley, followed by a second outstanding performance with 5A powerhouses Lancaster and Dallas Carter in their gym off Wheatland Road in South Dallas.

For those basketball lovers who have never experienced the fanaticism of a South Dallas arena, it is not for the weak-minded team or parent, but it can become an atmosphere of intimidation and errors. When the crowd chants "C.C., You Know," you instantly become aware that this environment is different. I totally appreciate the vibe that comes from our neighboring fans, and during the South Oak Cliff appearances around the Metroplex and Austin state tournament bids, that shout—"SOC, who you rooting for, SOC, who you rooting for"—was loud and captivating.

At Plano East, the squad is developing a following. Our shout-out is, "Plano Plano East East. It sounds so nice that we say it twice." The Plano East rally call will rival any of our southern programs, and our supporters are all knowledgeable. It is music to the ears when in the heat of battle.

Our team also welcomed a new follower/supporter, a friend of the program: Craig Smith, a basketball junkie, podcaster, YouTuber of 4The3Hoops, a local guy with a huge basketball following, came to East and sat down with Coach Wester for an interview.

Craig shared his thoughts, the style of play, and player-to-player analysis on why he thinks Plano East is the team to represent the region in San Antonio. And with the team camp, TABC showing, the GASO, and Carter Shootout, all of Texas became cognizant.

In six short years with Wester as the leader, the basketball program was lean and struggled the first season but has transformed from a 5–29 club to a highly competitive, state-contending representative.

When reminiscing, I think we were doing our best coaching but could not produce wins. The boys played their hearts out, followed the game plans, and many went over and beyond trying to improve their play, but victories were difficult to find. Adding to the double-edged sword was that our district was one of the deepest in 5A, with Allen, Denton Guyer, Wylie, and the Plano schools.

At times, the discouragement led to frustration, second-guessing marinated our thoughts, and personally, I witnessed tears forming in the eyes of both team members and coaches. The bus rides were longer, and the conversations lingered late into the night following lost games and often into early Wednesday and Saturday mornings. However, our grind was vigilantly surreal. There was more than enough arrogance, vision, and leadership in the coach's office to bring that needed change and direction for a championship title run.

The continued preparations of owning the opportunity, which began with the offseason weights and conditioning program, were to build the product from within. As a team, we don't look the part of a championship ball club. An average hoop fan could take a glimpse of the players and instantaneously place them into the overrated category. We aren't all that tall, don't appear to be athletic, and, less importantly, have no recognized Division I prospects.

A small goal was to construct stronger physical bodies, develop a mentally confident mindset, and be the best-conditioned group ever assembled at East. Our outward look may not be overwhelming, but our pound-for-pound strength and toughness will be the difference maker. It was discussed daily during workouts—what it is going to feel and look like when we walk into other gymnasiums. We want all eyes on us.

A clearer testament of dedication and camaraderie became more evident when the team completed our team individual and goals questionnaire one week prior to the season opener. Each player was asked a total of nine questions—three on self, three on team, and what can help or hurt the overall goal this year—then the team would gather and give accountability to their answers. The reading aloud forged a tighter bond.

Individual Goal = Have a bigger role on the team, become a better leader, start, average 10 points a game, etc. But everyone had the same team goal.

Team Goal = Win the State Title. And many had the audacity not only to write it on paper but to verbally communicate that they had the goal of going undefeated. The undefeated accomplishment has occurred twice in 5A—2020 during the shortened COVID season and in 2007, when Duncanville went 39–0—but not in the new revised 6A alignment.

2023–2024 Goals

Individual

1. Get a Division I Offer

2. Become more consistent

3. Gain a bigger role this season

Team

1. Win State

2. Compete at every practice

3. Break school record for wins

4. Go undefeated

Things I can Improve on?

1. Be More Aggressive

2. Body Language

3. My Defense

4. Finishing

What can I do to become a BETTER teammate?

1. Be more Vocal

2. Hold Myself/Teammates accountable

3. Bring Energy

4. Push Myself/Teammates

5. Lead By Example

What do you see that can become our team's Biggest Obstacle?

1. Selfishness

2. Getting Frustrated/Arguing with Teammates

3. Complacency

4. Outside Distractions

5. Not preparing

6. Not focusing

You can't CHEAT the grind.

It knows how much you invested. It won't give you anything you have not worked for.

Chapter VII

1st Quarter (The Streak Begins)

It seemed like the bus ride to North Crowley High took longer than what Google Maps estimated. Leo, a Plano East graduate and former player, who is enrolled at Collin County in the visual arts department and was given a class assignment—he parlayed it into becoming our team documentarian—videoed the entire season.

With all the first-game-of-the-year anxieties, nothing appeared to be out of whack. The gallery was relatively full of the normal hoop fans and spectators, but as we had prepared and discussed, all eyes turned to our players as we entered the gymnasium. People began to mumble, "Who is this?" a bystander asked. "Plano East," the other responded. I smirked at Xavier as he heard the conversation and tapped my shoulder. The team congregated at the end of the stands, on the bottom rows, to watch the current game before relocating to the assigned holding area until a locker room was available.

Over the years, it had become a common practice for the guys to watch the game in progress (junior varsity or tournament), shoot at the break point, return to the stands until the four-minute mark of the third quarter, then head to the locker room for our pregame preparations. However, this year, the routine was tweaked, and immediately after shooting, the team gathered their belongings and departed to the dressing area.

Our pregame change was to limit the possible distractions of friends, family, and spectators who wanted to see the state-ranked program. But the East rituals are a sight to witness. "I couldn't conceptualize this if I dreamt it myself." The creams and jelly, lotions, and mechanical devices they use to physically get ready for a competition are otherworldly. With the training room's medical smells and the noise from multiple drills (three or four at the same time) being utilized, the latest inventions for individual muscle relaxation and preparation—the mental image has one wondering, "How did we ever make it through a game, let alone a full season?" But for this group, it worked.

However, the early departure gave ample opportunity for all that craziness to subside and allowed the best coaching staff to offer our players the foremost scouting report on our opponent. I then went over everything detailed on the report, from personnel to what Durant or Irving shoes they had on their feet. How tall or short? Was the player left- or right-handed, his preferred shots, whether he defended, ran the floor, etc. Thanks to Coach Godwin and Coach Evans.

The review of the scout was detailed on each player. Their personnel was read aloud from the starters throughout their roster, along with our plan of attack or actions we needed to utilize for a positive outcome at the end of the game.

A visualization was exercised. Our players were directed to close their eyes and see themselves making game-winning plays, specifically against the team or player each would compete against that night. For example: Who is taking that charge? Who is diving on the floor for the loose ball? Who will block out, get a deflection, make that extra pass from a good shot to a great shot? Who is going to sacrifice himself for the team victory?

Tunes with a very specific message were played in the background.

The desired effect was spoken into existence.

Coach Wester entered the area, addressed the team with his vision, and delivered the finer points of his expectations. We circled up (1-2-3 Eastside, 4-5-6 State Champs) and exited the room.

Our warmup routine was specifically designed to be purposeful and efficient. In the 12–15 minutes, the time frame provided a good sweat to develop while the players had ample opportunities to find their rhythm and see the ball going through the net. The goal was to have each player attempt 100 shots at game speed.

- Layup (both sides) – 12 shots, midrange jumpers – 12 shots
- First Action – approx. 20 shots, 3–4 minutes
- Motion Action – approx. 20 shots, 3–4 minutes
- Free Throws – shoot 2 and rotate, 10–12 shots, 3–4 minutes
- 3-pointers – approx. 20 shots, rotating in 3 spots, 3–4 minutes, every 30 seconds

It's Game Time

First game of the season, #8 Plano East vs. #10 Allen, in the Cowtown Tip-Off at North Crowley High School. Two formerly district campuses separated by six miles traveled 62 miles, a bit more than an hour's drive, for an early matchup between two of the state's top 10 ranked ball clubs.

Iron sharpens iron, and this battle was worth the price of admission. An even square-off in the first quarter, 16–15 East, but Allen took a five-point lead into the half at 37–32. Allen's lead grew to ten points at the midpoint in the third before we physically upped our play and defensively took control of the game by pressing the ball handlers and holding them to one shot. East dominated the fourth quarter by a score of 24–13, eventually pulling away with a decisive 10-point margin win.

Allen 70 – Plano East 80

Allen: Thomas 18 pts, Walls 14 pts, Meyers 11 pts, Pane 9 pts, Lawrence 9 pts.

East: DJ 23 pts, Narit 23 pts, Xavier 10 pts, Rachard 7 pts.

(Reserves accounted for 34 pts).

East 1–0

"Well guys," I quipped to our coaching staff as the players continued to jump around the locker room, celebrating their victory with jerseys off and water splashing everywhere, "one down and thirty-nine games to go." Who knew! A swag was in the making.

Game 2 vs. Highland Park High School, East Home Opener

A return match of home and home and the opportunity to avenge the loss from one of the three programs that handed us a defeat last season. The Scots thoroughly whipped us on our visit to Dallas, and we (coaches) reminded the seniors on a regular basis. Of the five losses last season, East was never in the game. We had become comfortable with the early success and were completely and utterly embarrassed by the Highlanders last year. We were focused, prepared, and returned the favor with an easy home-opening victory.

Several seasons ago, Coach Wester changed the end-of-game procedure of shaking the opponents' hands and immediately going to the locker room for the coach roundup. He now encourages the guys to stay on the court after the final horn and socialize with the family and students. This method of showing appreciation to our supporters has increased the student body attendance and their participation during games.

East 70 – Highland Park 54
HPHS: Stribling 12 pts, Beckett 12 pts, Cantrell 11 pts, Saunders 8 pts.
DJ 26 pts, Narit 12 pts, Jon 10 pts. Every East player suited and played.
East 2–0

With the first of three tournaments, East entered the Dallas Mavs Fall Classic in Frisco, Texas, looking to play five games in three days. The team moved up three spots from the preseason #8 to #5 in the UIL, 3rd in the TABC, 2nd in GASO state rankings, and #4 in MaxPreps nationally.

Game 3 vs. International Leadership of Texas/Arlington @ Lebanon Trail High School, Mavs Tournament

The Panthers' Thursday Game #1 opposition was ILoTA, a charter school with players from Irving, Grand Prairie, and the Dallas area. We outclassed, outsized, and totally dominated the game from the toss to the last whistle. All fourteen East players entered the game, with five players scoring in double figures.

Plano East 92 – ILoTA 37

ILoTA: Smith 12 pts, Bradford 11 pts, Davis 8 pts, Jackson 6 pts. Izan 18 pts, Seth 15 pts, DJ, Xavier, Jon 10 pts each, Rachard 9 pts.

East 3–0

Game 4 vs. Walnut Grove @ Lebanon Trail High School, Mavs Tournament

Thursday, Game #2, was against upstart Walnut Grove High, out of Prosper, which provided a challenge with quick guards and tough play. The Panthers wore down the Wildcats as the game went on. Lesson learned today: how to properly approach trap games.

The main prerogative was to keep the guys focused on one game at a time, not looking ahead to the next game or opponent. This can be a challenge for a younger ball club, which we were not, but a challenge nonetheless. Our staff was aware of this phenomenon, and it was discussed frequently. Coach Wester preached being even-keeled—not too high and not too low.

Plano East 60 – Walnut Grove 45

WGHS: Evanson 22 pts, Scott 8 pts, Brooks 6 pts, Schaack 5 pts.

Xavier 16 pts, Jordan 15 pts, DJ 14 pts. Team: 15 assists, 14 steals, 17 deflections.

East 4–0

Game 5 vs. Lake Highlands High @ Centennial High School

Friday, day two of the Mavs Classic, featured a familiar opponent in Game #1. The bracket pairing provided East with an early mental and athletic challenge to avenge the heartbreaking playoff defeat that ended our season nine months ago. This was not a revenge game, but the opportunity to grow and prepare for the bigger picture was high.

The players had to learn how to win the psychological, as well as the physical and mental, aspect that comes with a game of this magnitude. This was early practice. Length and size did not factor much in this scrimmage. Tough defense and easy buckets, however, did. Both challenges were met, accepted, and delivered. The experienced squad was not easily rattled. Advantage East.

Coach Duffield, a Plano East alum, always fielded a competitive, skilled, tough squad, but our players were up for the task. Our defensive efforts caused problems for the Wildcats' young backcourt, and East won by 15.

Lake Highlands 47 – Plano East 62

LHHS: Moran 13 pts, DeMent 8 pts, Umeh 7 pts.

Jon 14 pts, DJ 14 pts, Xavier 10 pts, Jordan 9 reb, 3 stls.

East 5–0

Game 6 vs. Hebron @ Centennial High School

The second tournament game on Friday was against a respected district opponent, Hebron High. When the tournament bracket came out in September, Coach Godwin first noticed the matchup and texted our staff. It wasn't something any coach wanted to see scheduled, and it only occurs in tournament play—the rare possibility of facing a team three times in a single season.

Hebron played a formidable first half and managed to hit four deep, NBA-range threes behind the arc to keep the game within 10 points, 34–28, at the break. However, we achieved one of our team goals—to keep our opponent to 10 points or less in a quarter—and took control of the game with a smothering defensive effort in the third quarter, causing 14 points off turnovers and 12 points in transition.

The margin of victory wasn't the true representation of the game, both teams battling it out on every possession, with our guys' man-to-man defense making more plays. The next two games with Hebron would be exciting.

Hebron 53 – Plano East 70

Hebron: Haynes 23 pts, Toney 15 pts.

DJ 16 pts, Narit 13 pts, Xavier 11 pts, Isaiah 8 pts and 9 ast. Team had 11 deflections.

East 6–0

Game 7 vs. Mount Pleasant (5A State Ranked #5), Championship Game

The Tigers posed a defensive threat with two big, long centers and a pair of athletic, taller guards. Defensively, the plan was to take either their forwards or the guards away and make them one-dimensional. The defensive plan was executed to perfection, and our pressure on their primary ball handlers caused chaos early and often. Mount Pleasant was held to 9 points in the first quarter and 23 points at the break.

An energized East sprinted to a commanding 22–10 third quarter, leading 55–35 as the horn expired. A great team victory for the first championship of the season. Every player participated.

Plano East wins the Dallas Mavericks Tournament Championship.

Plano East 61 – Mount Pleasant High 45

MPHS: Webster 21 pts, Chism 8 pts, Smith 7 pts.

Jordan 16 pts, Jon 8 pts, Narit 8 pts, Rachard 8 pts, Isaiah 7 pts, DJ

6 pts.

DJ received Tournament MVP; Xavier and Isaiah were named to the All-Tournament Team.

East 7–0, State Rankings: TABC #3, UIL #3

Game 8 vs. Rowlett @ Rowlett

Rowlett offered very little resistance, and every East player that made the trip received court time. The score was 21–9 after one, 40–16 at the half. The defense was becoming our standard, our staple. The goal of keeping teams under 40 wasn't achieved, but for the second game in a row, holding an opponent to 45 points was respectable. East dominated the paint, scoring 48, more than half the total.

Rowlett 45 – Plano East 89

RHS: Urune 14 pts, Douglas 10 pts, Murray 8 pts.

Jordan 16 pts, Jon, Rachard, Narit 8 pts each, Isaiah 7 pts, 4 ast, 2 stl.

East 8–0

Game 9 vs. Springdale, Arkansas @ Duncanville (Thanksgiving Hoopfest)

Coach Wester received a late invitation to participate in the renowned Duncanville Thanksgiving Hoopfest at the Sandra

Meadows Memorial Arena. The players had mentioned wanting to participate if the opportunity ever arose—something that every high school basketball junkie in the Metroplex dreams of.

The excitement and the opponent didn't factor into the early equation. Just the recognition of being chosen to play in the event was a gigantic achievement for our basketball program.

The guys began to speak about playing on center court, under the state banners that hang high above for all to see, against prep teams like Montverde Academy, Riviera Prep, or St. Michael's (NY). A possible matchup against host Duncanville also flooded the locker room.

Isaiah and Xavier gave a prognostic stab that our opponent would be a prep adversary, but Jordan and Narit suggested it would be a public school. When the decision was announced, the fellas were mildly disappointed. Springdale High School, a state finalist in 2023 with two of their state's top players returning from our neighboring state of Arkansas, was the challenger.

But the major shock was that the game would not be played on center court, in front of the large crowd, with a commentator and live music, but instead in the reserve gym. The state's #3 ranked team was relegated to the smaller, auxiliary gym.

We, as coaches, were happy and frustrated at the same time. Major shade was shown to the Plano East basketball program, and that became another motivation for the team. The #MakingBelievers was birthed. The visualization was to physically dominate the man in front of you, deflect every pass, and dive on every loose ball. Be the best you today.

Make everyone—the fans, every local sportswriter and sport anchor, the podcasters, TABC, UIL coaches—take notice. Make a believer of every person that comes to watch our team play. Leave no doubt when the final buzzer sounds.

Springdale was the opponent, but Hoopfest was the adversary. The guys didn't need much in terms of channeling their emotions; however, I used this situation every time available. "They don't respect you" or "It's us against the world." "Embrace the target, wear it like a badge of honor," I said.

Within the group circle, our habitual rallying call of "Hard Work Pays Off" set the tone necessary for the day's competition. "1-2-3 Family, 4-5-6 State Champs" was bellowed out confidently. This was the new charge of the Panthers.

The game was never as close as on the tip. East took the first quarter 17–6 and the halftime break 33–12, eventually winning by 19. The Panthers achieved the team goal of 10 points or less in three quarters, holding down a talented state finalist team from Arkansas and managing to stifle their highly ranked Division I prospect to 10 points.

We were getting that swag about us, that unique blend of style, confidence, and attitude that the great players or teams possess. That brashness or cockiness which is needed when you play in these types of events. Our swag was in full effect as Springdale witnessed firsthand the Panthers' arrogance pulling in the same direction.

Springdale, Arkansas 34 – Plano East 53
SHS: Sealy 10 pts, Palmer 9 pts, Sims 5 pts.
DJ 14 pts, Narit 12 pts, Jon 12 pts, Xavier 6 pts.
East 9–0, Ranked #1 GASO, #2 UIL, #3 TABC, MaxPreps #7

As we exited Sandra Meadows Memorial Arena, I pulled the team together one last time and made a reference pointing upwards to their championship banners, adding fuel to our fire.

Game 10 – East vs. Waxahachie @ Waxahachie

Another long bus ride into a hostile environment, against another state-ranked team (fourth on the schedule), with a five-star prospect, proved its weight in gold—a term that dates back to the Roman dynasty—but neither the crowd nor the play on the court factored into the outcome of the game.

East took a commanding 24–5 first-quarter burst, followed with a 21–16 second quarter that gave the Panthers a 45–21 halftime lead. Waxahachie never threatened. A missing ingredient, thus far in the early season, resurfaced as Jordan's unique ability (for a 6'2" guard) to rebound the basketball sparked a five-point run with his two offensive putbacks and a free throw midway through the second quarter. His knack for getting to the ball is our secret weapon, the team's difference-maker. DJ had a double-double.

Plano East 81 – Waxahachie 50
WHS: Nunn 18 pts, Jefferson 12 pts, Gatewood 11 pts.
DJ 16 pts, Jordan 15 pts, 5 reb, 5 ast, Rachard 12 pts, Xavier 9 pts.
East 10–0

However, the atmosphere was just what the team needed. The idea of using the padded, individual seating in front of the visiting and home stands had not been contemplated. This gave us coaches some thoughts for our Archie McAfee Gymnasium and by far was the biggest takeaway from the contest. Creating a special area for our guests and VIP personnel would make an awe-inspiring memory. A visual we could use to hype the Jungle (student section) and enhance the home court advantage for the senior and alumni night festivities.

Game 11 – East vs. McKinney Boyd @ Boyd High

Rematch of 1st round playoff game last season

Plano East Ranking: UIL #2, TABC #2, GASO #2, MaxPreps #7

McKinney Boyd played a tough, hard-nosed, aggressive man-to-man defense. In this kind of contest, we had to match their efforts and intensity—not only on the floor but also with the energy from the cheering section. They were loud and obnoxious and, quite frankly, entertaining. The filth and abnormal overtones from their students could be bothersome to a younger team, and the chant "Overrated!" is now spouted by every student-led section we visit, which is to be expected. Our players eat it up like gummy bears.

A big opening quarter and a resilient fourth quarter gave East a hard-fought 10-point road victory. Again, Coach Wester demonstrated trust as every player entered the game.

Plano East 55 – McKinney Boyd 45
BHS: Hansen 11 pts, Brown 7 pts, Phillips 6 pts.
Jordan 20 pts, 6 reb, 5 stl, DJ 11 pts, Narit 10 pts. Xavier injured his wrist.
East 11–0

Game 12 – East vs. Rockwall @ Rockwall High

This was the fourth consecutive road game against a former district champion and a four-star prospect. To add to the challenge, starting point guard Xavier would not compete due to a wrist injury. Among this group of players, the next-man-up mentality was ever present. Narit stepped in, and the band played on. A huge kudos to Rachard as he rounded himself into that Swiss Army knife he is.

East won the first three quarters scoring 24, 14, and 11, while holding the Yellow Jackets to 9, 6, and 6—all under the team defensive goal mark of 10 points or less in a quarter. Taking a commanding lead of 49–21 into period four, Rockwall won the last quarter 16–15. A dominating victory. Scoring with ease, with a great defensive effort of not allowing the opponent more than 10 points in a quarter, was indisputable.

Plano East 64 – Rockwall 37
Rockwall: Turner 10 pts, Young 8 pts, Goellner 7 pts.
DJ 17 pts, Jordan 16 pts, Rachard 15 pts, Isaiah 4 reb, 3 ast, 5 defl, 1 stl.
East 12–0

'Most people have the will to win.'

'Few have the will to prepare to win.'

- Coach Robert "Bobby" Knight -

Chapter VIII

2nd Quarter (Tournament Play)

For the last 15 or more years, I have made a trip to the hills of northwest Arkansas for the red/white spring activities, a reunion, or to participate in something relating to my adoptive Razorback family. A few gatherings have been better than others, but this adventure was all about business. A biblical verse states that "pride comes before the fall," and I'm very prideful. Bringing our East ball club to the Fayetteville showcase is huge, personally and professionally.

Thursday morning did not arrive too soon. As the coaches (Godwin, Wester, myself) gathered in front of McAfee Gym, each with a sports utility vehicle rented for the next three days as the team traveled to Fayetteville, Arkansas, for the second tournament of the season—*Hoopin' in the Hills*—something I had been working toward, even orchestrated and begged for (an invitation) dating back four or five years. This tournament had been interrupted recently by COVID from 2021–2023, but we had an "in": three decades of friendship with Head Coach Brad Stamps and Assistant Coach Nick Bradford would be to our advantage.

Rebecca and I visited with Coach Stamps and Bradford in the spring of 2023 during my book tour. We shared an interest in participating in the Fayetteville High basketball tournament if it were to be reinstituted. I shared that we (East) had finished 31–5, lost to the eventual state champions, Lake Highlands, and would bring a solid senior squad that could be ranked as high as #1 or #2 in Texas. I also added a little nugget: an ask that they invite Lee's Summit West High and Coach Schieber, out of Kansas City, to the competition.

Over the years, while following this tournament, Lee's Summit had either won or played in the championship multiple times. The biggest gift would be that my college football teammate and close friend, Limbo Parks, would make the trip as Schieber's assistant.

Limbo posted about the Fayetteville tournament, bragged of their accomplishments, and gave me the biggest challenge: "You guys don't want none of Kansas City. Naw, naw, Texas ain't ready," Limbo stated. "We are definitely ready."

The trip into northwest Arkansas was the reward to the seniors for their hard work and dedication during the last two years. It was also an opportunity to play against quality opponents from four surrounding states, with different athleticism, styles of play, and a shot clock. And not to mention, a visit to a Division I Southeastern Conference campus, the University of Arkansas—my school.

After the booster parents arranged breakfast and snacks for the players, everyone gathered their belongings for an 8:30 departure and piled into the three sports utility vans for the five-hour drive to Arkansas.

This Arkansas tournament was the first opportunity, as a basketball program, to travel outside the great state of Texas and hopefully could provide a deeper bonding experience and growth for the ball club. I also reached out to a former local coach and extended a small invitation to attend the Friday night game, if available.

The schedule was as such:

- Depart Plano East between 8:30–8:45
- 11:30 Lunch in Sallisaw, Oklahoma (Subway)
- 1:00 Arrive at Van Buren High School (shoot-around)
- 2:45 Depart Van Buren
- 4:00 Arrive at Holiday Inn Express, Fayetteville, Ark.
- 6:00 Depart for Fayetteville High
- 8:00 Game vs. Putnam City High School, Oklahoma

Coach Godwin made the necessary arrangements for lunch at Subway in Sallisaw, Oklahoma, a small town off Interstate 40 and about one hour away from Van Buren, the site for the team practice. The guys welcomed the restroom break, the time to stretch, and to let off some steam. The stop was short and productive: a hot meal and togetherness.

With fourteen boys, similar interests, and shared goals, it can be a chore to keep them from fracturing off, but they know how to unwind. I've witnessed—and actually was a part of—some crazy phenomenon, but as I pushed the key to start the engine, I heard my van, all of them (Ethan, Jordan, Rachard, Xavier), begin to clap and loudly sing the words to the pop song *Party in the U.S.A.* by Miley Cyrus. "I could not believe my ears nor unsee with my eyes," but it was cool that they were this comfortable with one another.

I made a call to the head coach of Van Buren High, Brad Autry, the next destination on this adventure. Coach Autry and I met when he was an assistant college coach at the University of Arkansas–Little Rock (UALR) and he visited Plano East while recruiting the DFW area. We have stayed in contact, and when searching for a practice facility, another coach mentioned the new Van Buren gymnasium as a recommendation and asked if I knew Brad.

Excited for the chance to reconnect, I immediately scrolled down my contacts and texted him. After two rings Brad answered, and familiarity took over. We must have conversed for an hour, sharing old war stories on players and coaches, before I got around to asking about the availability of his gym next month, and he instantly replied, "Yes, what day and time?"

The caravan, with my wife Rebecca in tow, arrived in Van Buren, Arkansas, and after Google Maps took the group on a scenic route, we arrived at the Clair Bates Arena located on the east side of Van Buren High School's campus. The facility, built in 2009, seats approximately 2,000, has four locker rooms, two team rooms, multiple storage spaces, and a gigantic 20' x 50' big screen on the south wall and a four-face scoreboard from NEVCO. An absolute gem.

We arrived at 12:55 and quickly threw on the practice gear for a shoot-around. This exercise routine is what we utilize when in playoff preparation. Everything is aimed toward the march to San Antonio. I introduced Coach Autry to Wester, Godwin, Smith, and Rebecca, we took a few photos, and then went straight into practice.

A small group of their basketball team, boys and girls, sat about to watch as the guys equally divided up and began the daily shooting stations. Coach Autry introduced me to his team, and we talked for a brief moment. Someone asked, "How good are we?" I answered that we were undefeated and currently ranked #2 in Texas, but after this weekend and in two weeks, that could be updated when we play Stony Point, the #1 ranked team. Then the group dispersed and headed to class.

After the last horn buzzed, the team gathered at center court, walked over, and thanked Coach Autry for allowing them access to the gym, changed clothes, and off to the parking lot they went. Another hour's drive remained before we reached the final destination point, the infamous Holiday Inn Express—but only in the hills of Fayetteville, Arkansas.

We arrived at Holiday Inn Express shortly after 4:00 p.m., a little tired from the drive and happy to lay down on a bed for a couple of hours. The team was provided eight rooms for the players, two for the coaches, and a room for Rebecca and me. After everyone got checked in, the coaches briefly met in Godwin's room to get familiarized with the evening itinerary.

The team meeting, scheduled in the lobby for 5:45, was pushed back so that the players could double-check their backpacks and personal belongings for the night's competition. After the check-ins, the team congregated in the foyer before departing for Fayetteville High Gymnasium at 6:07 p.m.

Something I expressed to the guys, and it began early on during the offseason workouts, was whenever they were to enter a gym or the court, I wanted every head to turn and each eye to be on them. "Walk in with a swag, a pure sense of confidence, not cockiness— earned from knowing that the hard work is paying off—and let them ALL see it on display. Accept the attention that comes with being the #2 ranked team in Texas. Wear this recognition like it is a badge, an honor, to be in this position. You are worthy, with something to prove."

Hoopin' on the Hill, after a short hiatus due to a national health emergency, returned under new management, and the main sponsor, Big Chicken—furnished by NBA Hall of Famer Shaquille O'Neal—added appeal and brand recognition.

Game 13 @ Fayetteville, Arkansas vs. Putnam City High, Oklahoma (*Hoopin' on the Hill*)

Putnam City entered the tournament ranked in the top 10 of the Oklahoma High School Coaches Poll at #6, and with Plano East's #2 Texas ranking, this engagement, when paired in September, had the makings of a shootout. Nonetheless, as expected, we jumped out fast, hitting on all cylinders with an early 10–2 run and taking a 24–9 lead in the first quarter. East stymied a potent Putnam City squad, holding them to 6 points in both the second and third quarters, under 10 points in three of four periods, totaling just 21 entering the final stanza. East won the first-round game in dominating fashion. Every East player received court time.

Plano East 67 – Putnam City, Oklahoma 37
PCHS: Constant 13 pts, Rayfield 12 pts.
DJ 15 pts, Narit 13 pts, Jordan 6 pts, 9 reb, 3 ast, Isaiah 5 reb, 6 ast,

2 stl.

East 13–0

After a long day of travel, which included a divided five-hour drive broken up between a late lunch, an afternoon practice, check-in, and then an 8:00 p.m. tip-off, the guys were exhausted—but they were troopers. Their ability to focus is like no other team I've been around in my 20 years of coaching.

The night ended with each player receiving a large pizza from the local Domino's and a shake of their choosing from McDonald's, provided by my wife Rebecca. Lights out at midnight.

Friday morning anxieties began with an early wake-up call at 7:30 a.m. and an 8:00 team meeting in the lobby to discuss the tentative plan and activities. There were whispers that the 19-year NBA veteran, four-time world champion, three-time Finals MVP, and sports analyst on TNT's *Inside the NBA* would be in attendance—but it was only rumored. I attempted a second phone call. It went directly to voicemail, but that was understandable. Just knowing a message was left gave some hope that, if available, the best surprise of the weekend might come to pass.

The members and coaches reassembled in the lobby for the 8:45 departure to the University of Arkansas' Bud Walton Arena, the first of two scheduled tours arranged by Razorback track Hall of Famer

Randy Coleman—a two-time All-American, three-time national champion, former president and current board member of the Black Alumni Society, and a brother/friend. He is also one of only two HOF inductees who came to the Razorback family as a walk-on participant, the other being Brandon Burlsworth.

Randy is at the forefront and is doing a fabulous job of staying connected with former Razorback athletes while providing opportunities for local appearances, tailgating, guest interviews, and other participation in area events and activities. He also assigned Jazz Grewal, a graduate assistant in student-athlete development, as the tour guide for D.W. Reynolds Razorback Football Stadium. "As if I wasn't familiar—but the facility is closed to the public and no one is allowed to walk the grounds without supervision."

After a short scenic drive from the IHG, the empty parking lot gave an indication that the arena might not be open, and the pace of the guys from the SUVs was slower than usual. The early morning wake-up call, coupled with a chill in the air, left a few guys' thoughts on reserve concerning the morning's planned activities.

First, a team picture was taken outside Bud Walton Arena, "The Palace of Mid-America," built in 1993 with a capacity of holding 20,000 rabid, chanting Hog fans at every home stand. The doors were closed, so the group walked toward the University Bookstore located at the base of the arena. Like children in a candy shop, the guys scattered and began gazing at the Razorback attire. Here, everything has a pig or hog emblem on it. No Aggie. No Longhorn. No Tiger of any reference—not even a detergent box. Only the Razorbacks are sold.

The store manager was extremely energized as our group entered his establishment. Dollar signs must have flooded his thoughts as he witnessed an entourage of 20-plus possible future Razorback patrons walk through the entrance slightly after 9:00 a.m.

"Hello," he said. "My name is Robert. What can we do for you today?" He and his assistant smiled by his side. I reached out to shake his hand as I completed the greeting. "Morning, my name is Greg," I explained who we were. "I'm an assistant coach with Plano East Senior High basketball team. We're next door playing in the Fayetteville High tournament this weekend, and I wanted the players, family members, and coaches to get a look around Bud Walton."

Robert paused for a moment, then responded, "The facility is closed today. No games are scheduled, and both teams are on the road."

I whispered into his ear, "My name is Greg Thomas, former Razorback player," hoping it would provide some recollection or jog his memory. Several players and Assistant Coach Michael Godwin overheard my comment.

Robert replied, "Let me make a call."

Robert picked up the phone, dialed a number, and within seconds he stated, "Mr. Thomas, you have access to the facility. I'll unlock the doors and be your guide to the basketball and track museum for as long as you want. Please follow me."

I was somewhat taken aback; entrance was the goal, but a personal tour from the manager exceeded the request. Nonetheless, Robert turned on the lights, unlocked the large glass doors, and East entered the southern side of Bud Walton, the Razorback history of basketball and track.

Robert began with the statues of Razorback legends Mike Conley and Joe Kleine, both Hog Hall of Famers, Olympian winners, and friends. He led our group to the "Triplets" area but was summoned away as a shipment arrived and needed his immediate attention. I, however, picked up where he left off and continued down memory lane.

The "Triplets" referenced Coach Eddie Sutton's and Arkansas' first Final Four appearance in 1979 and was led by a trio of Arkansas-born members: Ron Brewer, Marvin Delph, and Sidney Moncrief, all with the same build, skill set, and style of play. They

105

are famously remembered within the borders of the "Natural State" for losing in the NCAA semifinals to the Indiana State Sycamores and Larry "Legend" Bird, the National College Player of the Year.

As the group navigated through the museum, Xavier called out, "Coach T., isn't this the guy we met last year at the In-N-Out Burger Allen Holiday Basketball Invitational?" Several had walked up to the trophy case that showcased Scotty Thurman's high-arching winning shot in the national championship game against Duke University. The entourage quickly followed Xavier's voice and congregated for a look. As I tried to explain to Isaiah and Jordan, "You were in the presence of royalty. He is a national champion."

Now the team was within feet of a national championship trophy, but I wanted to share a story or two about the man—the coach—who would lead the Razorbacks to the Mount Rushmore of collegiate basketball supremacy: Coach Nolan Richardson. I had their undivided attention.

"Are you familiar with the movie *Glory Road*, the Walt Disney picture about Texas Western College's defeat over the Kentucky Wildcats for the 1966 NCAA National Basketball Championship?" Almost each shook their heads yes, while a few verbally answered.

As they gazed at the picture of Coach, I shared the movie plot of Head Coach Don Haskins altering his lineup when he decided on starting five Black players (the first time in a championship game) against Kentucky's all-white ball club led by their legendary coach, Adolph Rupp.

Coach Richardson, a Texas Western College alum—now known as the University of Texas at El Paso—was recruited and played for the symbolic, historical decision-making Don Haskins, himself a Naismith Basketball Hall of Fame inductee in 2007, from 1961–1964.

The guys were accustomed to me channeling a Coach Richardson saying like, "You kill an ant with a sledgehammer" or "If you see me and a bear in a fight, you'd better help the bear," my intrepid attempt to provide a demonstrable visual of what is expected before today's competition. Each intently gazed at the picture of Richardson hoisting the national trophy over his head as I summoned them (individually and collectively) to visualize holding our state championship trophy over their heads, just as Coach Richardson had, three months from now.

The seeds had been planted several years ago. Today those seeds were being nourished.

All eyes were closed. No movement, no one saying a word. Only focused on the fantasy they could make happen. It will happen. The imagery occupied the brainbox. This was our reality to create: a reaffirmation of the team's ultimate goal. To be the last team standing, celebrating, hugging, and emphatically raising that wooden prize signifying the highest accomplishment completed—the UIL State Championship, on March 9.

Store manager Robert rejoined our group near the 2000s trophy case to continue the tour, but before long, our hour was up. The second round of the day's adventure awaited.

We exited Bud Walton for the cars, not wanting to challenge ourselves with the walk to D.W. Reynolds Razorback Stadium, approximately a half mile away. More time was lost leaving the parking lot than it would have taken if we had braved the walk.

A few of the players, as they were getting out of the SUV, noticed the huge water fountain to the left of the parking lot adjacent to the football stadium and began walking in that direction for a photo op. The bronze 20' x 30' water feature had six Razorback hogs, custom lighting, and was gifted by former Razorback and current Dallas Cowboys owner Jerry Jones.

We were a little early for the second tour Randy Coleman had arranged, and I was probably more excited—even emotional—because I had lived in this facility four decades ago. This area was also closed to the public, but Randy arranged for graduate assistant coach Jazz Grewal, of the Student-Athlete Development Department, to act as tour guide.

Jazz met our team outside D.W. Reynolds, and the first stop was in the Hall of Honor area, located inside and across from Hog Heaven Team Store. We then visited the Razorbacks' home and walk-on locker rooms. "You can play games in this room," Carter said. We ventured down the hall, but senior Chima decided to sit down in one of the huge lockers and briefly grinned. He was in the process of taking his college visits at several Division I campuses, Iowa and Kansas, but he had to admit he was a little in awe of what Arkansas presented.

Jazz then led everyone to the elevator, where we walked the hall to the field area. Before entering the north end zone, we all gathered for another photo shoot, then exited the doors to the playing field. I felt a few goosebumps formulating on my arms as the door opened and quick memories came flooding back. "I have these feelings every spring when my wife and teammates attend our annual reunion in April."

We ended the visit as Jazz led the group to Bowl Alley, the area of the stadium that honors all the Razorback teams, bowl history, and individual accomplishments. He stopped the guys in front of the season when I was the quarterback. Four consecutive years as a bowl team and a picture of me. Several players were stunned to see my image on the wall—a couple of coaches too—but it was there for all to see. I was honored that Jazz made this available.

The players were enlightened by two hour-and-a-half tours of the University of Arkansas basketball and football facilities before 11:30 a.m., finishing just in time for a quick lunch and a mid-morning shoot-around at Fayetteville High School.

Afterwards, it was back to the IHG for rest for a few hours before returning to the Fayetteville gymnasium for the nightcap with North Little Rock High, winners from yesterday's match vs. Oklahoma Douglass High, at 8:00 p.m.

Text sent and wake-up call to the players' rooms:

4:30 – Meeting in the Lobby
5:00 – Depart for Fayetteville High
5:15 – Arrive at Fayetteville High

As we entered Fayetteville High's *Bulldog Arena*, instantaneously a buzz formed in the area. Bewilderment with an urge of anticipation stirred the large crowd; all eyes were diverted toward our direction and the guys reciprocated that energy. I leaned over toward Jordan and Narit as they were taking a seat on the bottom bleacher. They uttered a comment that began in summer weight sessions, "I told you," with a huge grin upon their faces. "I told you this would happen." We could sense something in the air, and nothing out of the ordinary had occurred—just our entrance into the gymnasium seemed to spark everyone's excitement.

The coaches stood in the hallway outside the visitor locker room while the team watched the possible opponents for either the third-place game or, if we handled our business, the championship game to be played tomorrow at 3:00 p.m. Saturday.

Keeping the players in the moment was preached by Coach Wester. Maintaining an even keel was discussed on a regular basis. "That's what wins games. Never too high and never too low, always about right here," he demonstrated with his hand movement. However, this was the best team I had ever had the privilege to coach: they could play, joke around, act silly—what have you—and in a moment's notice they could pull everything together, zero in, and focus on the task at hand. They were the absolute best collection of players with this ability.

While in the locker room, as the team was changing out of the new gray travel sweats into their black uniforms with the gold lettering of "EAST" graphically positioned across the front of the jersey, during a stoppage of play music was blasted over the sound system and heard throughout the stands.

This oddly particular song, no matter what the players were doing—in practice, between timeouts of a game, or traveling—if it came over the airwaves, the guys (every member) chimed in. This out-of-character behavior overtook them. They, in unison, began to recite loudly and proudly, jumping up and down, actively engaged as if they were attending a live concert—to the words of Miley Cyrus' Billboard Hot 100 hit song *Party in the U.S.A.* "Are you kidding me? Not Eminem, or Drake, nor Kendrick Lamar, yet Miley Cyrus does this." It was inexplicable and absolutely entertaining to witness, and it summed up this group of players in a nutshell: FUN.

This song, *Party in the U.S.A.*, had become the unofficial Plano East team song.

After the song played out, the guys continued to dress and exited the locker room for the halftime shoot-around. A quick glimpse at the possible competitors or stretching for a few, as the clock displayed 3:45 remaining before the second-period conclusion.

I saw my wife, Rebecca, sitting with several of my college teammates in attendance who had come to support. Limbo Parks, who came with Lee's Summit West team and was the only reason Plano East had any knowledge of this tournament. Marshall "ROK" Foreman, and my two closest friends, Luther Franklin, Ritchie Miller, Anthony Hicks, and Micheal Porter, rounded out the bunch.

We were cutting it up when Rebecca tapped me on the shoulder as she noticed a small entourage entering the floor area to our left. "He made it, look Greg, Coach Richardson is here," Rebecca said.

The BEST surprise walked into *Bulldog Arena*.

Former Razorback Basketball Head Coach Nolan Richardson—the Basketball Hall of Fame inductee, national champion, NIT champion, NJCAA national champion, and my mentor—honored the request I sent out to him and graced our space with his presence.

"I'm stunned but not surprised. Coach has always championed and supported me." From the time we met in my youth, through my playing days as a Razorback, to being a participant in my autobiography, *No Doubting Thomas*, Coach had been a staple for me.

My movement was slow, attempting not to exhibit any urgency while desperately trying not to display the real emotional state that was growing inside. But the anxieties were beginning to manifest. *Are we ready to play? What will Coach think about our players?* These questions emerged as I moved nearer toward my real-time hero I had grown to admire and know. As I was walking in his direction, other basketball fans and coaches became cognizant of this rare appearance of Nolan Richardson, outside of Razorback home games from time to time, and looked eager and excited as a small crowd congregated around Coach. Garret, his grandson (designated driver for the day), and several of his great-grandchildren observed.

Eye contact was made with Garret as I approached the group when Coach was pulled slightly to his right in my direction. Shortly after, we embraced and greeted one another, like a teacher to his pupil. An extended handshake followed with a long hug. It wasn't as if we hadn't seen one another in a while—honestly, we do this several times a year at other Razorback functions or activities. But this was a first occasion.

Our phone conversations had me bragging on this collection of players, the real possibilities, and how he would be proud of them because we had adopted his defensive philosophies and style of play. I often used his pointed quotes as a motivational approach when addressing the members—no, establishing demands of them—to play harder for their teammates than they would for themselves.

For those who truly knew him, they could imagine the smirk on the face of Coach Richardson as he reminisced, slightly laughed, then commented, "If you guys play in the area, I will do my best to get out and watch you guys. I will need early notice, I have to be sure of the coverage for Mrs. Rose, but yeah, I'll be there."

Today was that day.

"Greg Thomas," Coach said, "I don't believe I've attended a high school game in, let's see, fifteen years. Maybe longer." He steadied himself behind the visiting bench. I motioned to our players to walk to this end of the court because the second period was winding down, and it was the norm for the next two teams to perform halftime shooting during the intermission.

The guys began to make their way from the bleachers onto the court area as I walked Coach Richardson to the players. They formed a single line for a brief meet-and-greet, a handshake with the Hall of Fame icon, my coach of coaches, Nolan Richardson. Our coaching staff—Matt Wester, Micheal Godwin, and Jamie Smith, the Camden, Arkansas native—were all astonished. Each player and coach had the opportunity to speak with Coach Richardson and to take a photo. I videoed the entire occurrence, then we returned to the locker room for the pregame scouting report on North Little Rock High, the day's opponent at 8:00.

All the dominoes were lining up. The team, truth be told, had an interestingly long day—with two tours and meeting a national champion coach—yet still had a job to do. That was why they were in another state, 5½ hours from home: a game to play.

North Little Rock didn't know what they were in for. Coach Richardson, Garret, and the boys took up residence behind our bench, two rows up. I noticed because I was watching his every movement, not wanting the guys to misstep or fail to achieve a team goal. They wanted Coach to be in full view of their dominance, in the form of his teaching: great defense and easy buckets.

Game 14 vs. North Little Rock High @ Fayetteville, Arkansas (*Hoopin' on the Hill*)

Plano East again dominated the first quarter, racing out to a 21–11 lead with a stifling, suffocating defense and an unstoppable inside presence. NLR won the second period 15–13 but still trailed at the midpoint 34–26. However, the eight-point deficit felt like 18. East's combined finish in the third and fourth quarters, 22 in each, gave the Panthers the 44–34 advantage needed to make the championship game. East's depth was showing, as every Panther player saw the court.

Plano East 78 – North Little Rock 60
NLRHS: J. Withers 27 pts (the most points allowed individually thus far).
DJ 20 pts, Xavier 14 pts, Jordan 12 pts, Jon 8 pts, Narit 8 pts, Rachard 8 pts.
East 14–0

Like Thursday night's game, the custodians began cleaning *Bulldog Arena* halfway through the third quarter. Stands that had seated approximately 500 spectators before the 8:00 tip-off had emptied to fewer than 50 or so during the final stanza on consecutive evenings—not including the North Texas group of 20-plus East Side faithful, who traveled from Plano to provide support.

Game 15 vs. Fayetteville High @ Fayetteville, Arkansas (*Hoopin' on the Hill*)

The Championship Game.

Following a light dinner, the team arrived at Holiday Inn Express before 10:00 p.m. A quick meeting in Coach Wester's room allowed us to share thoughts on tomorrow's opponent—the host, Fayetteville High, and long-time friends Head Coach Brad Stamps and his assistant, Lance Jenkins.

A slew of video clips and player recognition were discussed, and emphasis was placed on getting rested for what could be a challenging game. Lights out at midnight was echoed among the team.

An expected hostile environment greeted the Panthers as we made our way from the parking lot into *Bulldog Arena*. The cross representation of students, football players, and local fans packed the home side portion of the gym.

This was why this tournament was selected. Getting exposed to big, rambunctious, unrestrained, and overly cheerful crowds could pave the way for what it will be like as we make a run for San Antonio, the state tournament. Coach Wester's compilation of challenges and visiting arenas was exactly how he envisioned it.

What Coach did not foresee was my interaction with the boisterous pack of onlookers. I wandered over to the fandom and began to chop it up. "Who did you come out to see?" I asked. Out of the corner of his eye, Coach Wester witnessed my approach to the student body, then looked toward my wife Rebecca and motioned to her, "What is he doing?" Rebecca responded by shaking her head.

I asked the gathering again, "Who did you guys come to see?" A few commented, "We came to watch DJ."

"Which DJ, #0 for us?" I quipped.

They replied, "No, #9 for FHS."

I shot back, "You guys are about to get embarrassed! You do know that we are the #2 ranked team in Texas, and we will be ranked #1 by the end of the month. You are aware of this, yes?"

They smiled and laughed at my statement. One student replied, "We gonna' kick your butts."

I grinned, almost walked away, then turned as if I hadn't forgotten my reason for going over to their student section. "Congratulations, guys," I said to the football players in that area of the stands, "for winning the state championship of Arkansas." I followed the compliment with, "Now watch how the next state champions in Texas basketball do it," and walked back onto the court to conclude our pregame shooting drills.

As I strolled toward our bench area, taking a leisurely gallop around the chairs, Coach Wester asked, "What did you say to the home crowd? You have them all riled up?"

I replied, "Congratulated them on their football state championship and told them to buckle up—we're about to whip their boys' tails."

Fayetteville got out to an early four-point lead and stretched it to five before our guys settled in, winning the first quarter 12–9. Then our defensive pressure amped up, and we took total control for the remaining three periods. We won the second quarter 17–7, the third 19–6, and the fourth 23–8. For the third straight day, the stands emptied to fewer than 100 occupants—mostly outnumbered by East supporters. The Panthers cemented the game early in the third period. Every member saw court action as we captured the reinstalled *Hoopin' on the Hill* Championship in *Bulldog Arena* against host Fayetteville High. A balanced scoring attack along with a hawking defense was the difference.

That SWAG was real.

Fayetteville 33 – Plano East 70
Fayetteville: DJ Hudson 9 pts, Xavier Brown 6 pts.
Isaiah 13 pts, DJ 9 pts, Izan 9 pts, Ethan 7 pts, Jordan 7 pts, Xavier 6 pts.
Jordan was named Tournament MVP and earned a Shaquille O'Neal framed jersey.
DJ and Isaiah were named to the All-Tournament Team.
East 15–0

After a brief celebration with family and travelers, we quickly loaded the vehicles for the long drive home to Plano. Coach Wester's goal for the trip to Fayetteville: play and win a tournament in a hostile, challenging environment; reward the senior class for their commitment to the program; provide a deeper bonding experience among the members; and prepare the team for a playoff run.

Mission accomplished.

About an hour out, the players chose Popeyes for the victory meal, and we pulled over in Van Buren, Arkansas. More bonding—or better yet, decompressing—was needed. A major chip was emphatically knocked off the proverbial block.

"The guys just delivered a dominant weekend performance against some quality ball clubs and quite possibly could be ranked #1 by either the Texas High School Coaches Association or the University Interscholastic League, or both," Coach Godwin commented. But we knew this recognition would be decided at the end of the month when we met up in the CBI Tournament (formerly the Whataburger), if Stony Point took care of business on their end.

It's "ALL" in the Journey.

The process is only valued when your hard work is delivered.

Chapter IX

3rd Quarter (District 1st Round)

Following one day of rest and still on an emotional high, Monday's preparation for Flower Mound Marcus High, our first district adversary, began sluggishly and frustrating. The celebration from the weekend triumph in Arkansas was fresh on their minds, and the fellas ate it up. It was a well-earned outcome, but mature teams, like this squad, should handle success better and approach the next opponent as a capable and dangerous team—a hungry group eager for a bite of the apple against a state-ranked team, and in a district game to boot.

FM Marcus is what sports columnists deem a trap opponent: a good team that can beat anyone on any given day if not properly prepared for or overlooked.

With Coach Wester driving the bus, multiple players in the training room, and a few others making up tests for classes missed the previous Friday, chaos best described the scene. As people trickled in, all continuity was lost, which led to a lack of concentration and a "go through the motions" participation. Coach Wester's attempts to change the mood or players' current state of mind took several stations before he abruptly summoned everyone downstairs to his classroom for film study. The displeasure was visible on his face.

The walk from the court to the basement, honestly, was a welcomed blessing and gave a restart to practice. A stop by the restroom and a swig of water allowed the guys to refocus their efforts and adjust their passive attitudes with regard to the practice plan. "Nothing like the eye in the sky. It sees everything." And, like my college quarterback coach David Lee would say, "The camera has a way of humbling a person."

Game 16 – Flower Mound Marcus vs. East @ Plano East

East managed to take advantage, 35–27 at the half, due to Marcus' lack of inside presence, but the Marauders kept the game close with timely shooting beyond the arc. The Marauders shot 48% for the game, 11 of 13 from the free throw line, and 10 of 29 behind the three-point line (doubling East's makes/attempts) but still fell short. Jordan's double-double followed up his MVP weekend in Arkansas.

Getting back into a routine was the next best thing for our players. "We didn't shoot it well and gave up on loose balls, allowing second-chance scoring. Both can and will be addressed," Coach Wester said in the locker room roundup.

Plano East 65 – Flower Mound Marcus 61

FM Marcus: Ramnaman 20 pts, Susko 12 pts, Dudley 12 pts.

DJ 15 pts, 9 reb, Narit 14 pts, Jordan 12 pts, 13 reb, Xavier 9 pts, Isaiah 9 pts.

East 16–0, District 1–0

Friday night, December 15, couldn't get here fast enough— Round 1, the road matchup between two highly contested, state-ranked district nemeses: Plano East and Lewisville High, on the campus of Lewisville High.

This contest could play heavily in determining the pairing should both teams qualify for the state tournament at the end of the regular season. But neither team, the coaches, nor the fans were thinking that far in advance. An old-school, knock-'em-on-the-butt style of game was the rule, not the exception. With East winning five of the last six meetings, both squads entered this contest undefeated—East with 16 wins and the Farmers 15–0, ranked by GASO #2 and #8 respectively.

Lewisville Head Coach Toby Martin has always fielded a competitive, energetic team with a style of play not often matched, and this team was very impressive. Coach Godwin's scouting report reflected their pressure-on-the-ball ability and the isolation, one-on-one offensive style they offered, which could spell disaster if we couldn't handle their press or take care of the ball.

This early district challenge against a very good team, in a raucous gymnasium, with great fan support and a terrific coaching staff, was what basketball fanatics dream about. The possible ramifications for the unsuccessful squad could be massive. But this opportunity was exactly what we'd been preparing our players for since that Tuesday night in late February, at Moody Coliseum, ten months ago.

The players, however, were quite jovial and relaxed. Truthfully, the guys weren't too concerned about the group in the other side of the locker room. An aura of invincibility permeated the room.

"In order to be the best, one must defeat the best." A coach-speak reference.

Challenge accepted.

Game 17 – East #2 vs. Lewisville #8 @ Lewisville High School

The Farmers' gymnasium witnessed an evenly matched shootout, with East winning three quarters after a 15–15 duel in the first stanza. East's defensive dominance in the second period was the knockout blow. The 21–4 result came from tough man-to-man, smothering defense and an efficient scoring effort to take control at the half, 36–19.

East's balanced attack had six players in double figures while Lewisville had four.

This was Rachard's, senior guard, coming-out party. His energy and aggressive attacks downhill set the tone for the game. *Friday Night Glory* reporter Kenny Matthews interviewed co-captains Jordan and Isaiah near center court at the conclusion of the game.

Plano East 84 – Lewisville 63
Lewisville: Chambers 20 pts, Brown 14 pts.
DJ 16 pts, Jordan 15 pts, Isaiah/Narit 12 pts, Jon/Rachard 10 pts, Miller 7 pts.
East 17–0, District 2–0

After a needed week off because of end-of-semester testing and final exams, the guys—exhausted from scrimmaging with and against the sub-varsity—looked forward to the next tournament opponent: Birdville High, in the CBI (Championship Basketball Invitational), formerly known as the Whataburger Tournament, with an eye on the real possibility of the top two ranked 6A basketball programs squaring off for the #1 ranking and bragging rights in the great state of Texas. Plano East was vying for state and national recognition.

The team was extremely excited about earning the invite to the CBI and proving they deserved the right to play top-notch opponents like Leander Rouse and Stony Point. "We want that #1 ranking," Xavier commented.

East's last invite to the CBI (Whataburger) dated back some ten seasons ago in 2013–2014, with East's best appearance coming in the championship game vs. California Long Beach Poly High in 2012–2013, losing 51–40.

The CBI is at the top of the heap when tournament invitations are offered. To receive this invite, sportswriters, state basketball aficionados, and a board of former coaches must think your ball squad is something to be reckoned with and worthy of being showcased on the biggest stage at the midpoint of the season. "As a team, we've worked extremely hard to get an invite to this tournament. We earned this opportunity," Isaiah stated.

Game 18 – East vs. Birdville High @ Mansfield Legacy High, CBI Tournament Game #1

The long bus ride to Mansfield did little to loosen up the anxieties within our players' minds. The musical playlist featured Sleepy Hallow's *Anxiety* to set the mental tone for the tournament.

Volleyball's idea of bringing a large speaker along on their away games was adopted, and I developed a specific array of artists and songs to energize, motivate, and set the desired tone for that added edge. Certain lyrics can push the envelope.

Since the summer preseason game with Stony Point in the Coaches TABC, our players, individually and as a group, had looked forward to this possible matchup once the tournament field was announced.

They were built for this moment. They'd been on a training mission for three years. It was iron sharpening iron. Preparation and totally focusing in mentally was paramount.

Nevertheless, three games needed to be played and won if this #1 vs. #2—the state of Texas' and national top-ranked basketball clubs—were to square off. Both teams had to defeat a few other state-ranked opponents to qualify for this dream game.

Birdville was such a team. Year in and year out, district champions and playoff attendees, they were scheduled as the first game.

East jumped out with an early first-quarter lead, 28–11, applying multiple defensive schemes to confuse Birdville, forging a 54–25 halftime score. That Coach Richardson statement, "Kill the ant with a sledgehammer," was in full effect. The second half was similar, with East winning the third 15–7 and the fourth 21–12. We shot 54% from the field and 45% from deep while holding Birdville to 35% and 27%. We won the paint battle as well, outscoring the Hawks 46–16. Their zone defense was no match for our shooting. Every Panther contributed to the victory. The SWAG was real.

Birdville 44 – Plano East 90
Birdville: Warren 10 pts, Dotson 10 pts
Jon 15 pts, Narit 13 pts, Jordan 12 pts, Miller 11 pts, Moss 10 pts
East 18–0

Game 19 – Leander Rouse vs. East @ Mansfield Legacy High, CBI Tournament Game #2

A great matchup between top-ten opponents: 5A Leander Rouse, with two high-major Division I players, vs. 6A #2 Plano East. This was a battle from the tip. A hard-nosed defensive type of game was expected, with skillful shooting and athletic ability on display. Rouse took a 16–12 first-quarter lead, and East responded with an 11–7 second for a 23–23 halftime tie. They were the tougher team in the first half.

Coach Wester preaches the tougher team will win the game. "Tough players don't react." This was the first time this season Coach Wester truly challenged the players, and during intermission he did just that. We responded with an 18–11 third period behind a pair of Jon's three-pointers, and Narit sank two free throws with under three seconds, securing a four-point margin to hold off a fierce Leander Rouse comeback.

Plano East 51 – Leander Rouse 47
LRHS: Moore 15 pts, Gardner 13 pts, Haywood 11 pts
DJ 19 pts, Jon 10 pts, 5 ast, Narit 7 pts, 9 reb, 3 ast, Jordan 6 pts
East 19–0

"Great teams make adjustments, they don't react," Coach Wester preached. "They find a way to overcome situations and do the little things not recorded in the stat books: diving on the floor for loose balls, giving up the body for a charge taken, the extra pass from a good shot to a better shot. The minor sacrifice for a maximum result." Jon and Narit did those things.

HARD WORK PAYS OFF!

The momentum was building. They were learning what it takes to win—trusting the plan and having fun doing it.

#MakingBelievers

Immediately following the game, Coach Wester gathered the team, loaded the bus, and drove to Coach Lambert's house for lunch and relaxation. The tournament schedule allowed for about five hours before the next winners' bracket game, which would be played at 6:30. In most cases, the option would be to drive back to Plano, grab food and come back, watch a movie, or lay around the gym.

Coach Lambert offered his new residence, not far from the tournament site—which had a large TV screen and an even bigger swimming pool than his previous Parker, Texas, abode—for the players to relax. It was cold outside, but the guys enjoyed the jaunt. A good meal, Xbox football challenges, and a dip into the freezing water turned out to be just what the basketball gods ordered.

While the coaches ate and napped, the players loosened up and entertained themselves outside. The cold shock of the swimming pool, hypothermia, and numbness was likened to our weekly ice bath I administered for our players every Wednesday after practice. After a dip in the water, Isaiah, Carter, and Rachard quickly made their way to the hot tub. Two hours later, refreshed and ready, the team returned to Legacy High.

Game 20 – Arlington Martin vs. East @ Mansfield Legacy, CBI Tournament Game #3

Powered with a great defensive presence, along with paint dominance from DJ and pinpoint shooting from guard Jon (7/9 from the field, leading the team in scoring with 20 points), the Panthers took a 20–10 lead after one and a commanding halftime advantage, 34–15, over an outmanned Martin High. More evenly matched sparring in the third and fourth quarters permitted East an easy victory and established for the CBI Tournament Committee their dream championship matchup: the Plano East Panthers vs. the Round Rock Stony Point Tigers.

Plano East 73 – Arlington Martin 47

Martin: Warren 16 pts, Mitchell 15 pts, Groce 6 pts

Jon 20 pts, DJ 17 pts, 10 reb, Jordan 14 pts, 7 reb, 4 ast, Xavier 9 pts, Isaiah 7 pts

East 20–0

The CBI (Championship Basketball Invitational) committee's dream match between the state's #1 and #2 ranked teams—and among the National MaxPreps Top 25—Round Rock Stony Point and Plano East, became the most anticipated tournament showcase in the country. The game was televised on NFHS and featured Josiah Moseley of Stony Point, the #1 player in Texas, vs. DJ Hall, the up-and-coming junior for Plano East.

But this game would have more plots and subplots: coaching philosophy vs. style of play, physicality vs. skill sets, referee charters, game adjustments, and managing personnel. Gamesmanship at its finest.

Game On...

The plan, like every other game thus far, was to prove the doubters wrong. "We have been doubted the whole season. People don't like us, Plano East. Our name is said wrong all the time. We live through those doubts and rise to the occasion every time. It's nothing new to us," Rachard stated.

This is the challenge that all great teams must go through. In order to be the champ, you have to defeat the champ. If you want to be recognized as the best basketball team in the state of Texas, you have to defeat the team ranked #1—Stony Point—the team that holds the spot above you.

This seed was planted two years ago, in the revolving weight rooms of our high schools, McMillen and Williams, during Plano East's roof renovations, and on the track of East during the hot summer mornings.

Making Believers was becoming the team theme; proving it on the court became the mission. It was us against everybody else: the sporting people, the competition, the fan base, even our friends. The course had long been laid out, and a belief system paced on its course.

"We are labeled as a hardworking, family-oriented group who have been working together since middle school trying to accomplish something that hasn't been accomplished: going 40–0 before," Jordan explained in an interview following the Rouse game.

They believed now. The schedule Coach Wester put together, the shootouts we attended, the tournaments we chose to participate in—these established a shift in expectations and provided the confidence necessary to play in a game of this magnitude. Today's game was only proof of what was to come.

Game 21 – Stony Point #1 vs. Plano East #2 @ Mansfield Legacy, CBI Tournament

The Championship Game.

Stony Point entered this game 21–0 with victories in the tournament vs. Coppell High, Keller High, and South Grand Prairie High. All were ranked programs with phenomenal coaches and players with championship pedigree.

This matchup was all that and more. From the tip, the game began as a trading-baskets affair. Plano East took a two-point lead following the tip after one pass, but a backcourt violation call wiped away the score because the teams had lined up incorrectly. A timeout corrected the referee mishap, and East went on to take an 11–9 lead after period one.

Tough defense from both teams, with timely three-pointers from Stony Point, kept the game close. East led by five at half, 25–20. Stony Point won the third stanza 20–14 behind Landon Short's deep-ball shooting, giving the Tigers a 40–39 lead at the end of the third quarter.

East's stifling defense returned the favor in the final period as seniors Jordan, Narit, and Xavier's clutch shooting made the difference. With the score 54–50 and six seconds remaining on the clock, Isaiah, fouled in desperation, received the ball from the referee. Signaled for one shot, he went through his charity stripe routine, and in what retrospectively seemed like slow motion, calmly launched the game-sealing free throw.

East won the battle of #1 vs. #2. The win positioned the Panthers to become recognized as the best high school basketball team in the state of Texas for the first time in school history.

Plano East 55 – Stony Point 50
Stony Point: Short 20 pts, Moseley 12 pts, Goodlet 10 pts, Cruz 7 pts
DJ 18 pts, 5 reb, 3 def, 2 stl, Narit 12 pts, 12 reb, Isaiah 12 pts, 5 reb
DJ Tournament MVP; Jordan and Narit All-Tournament
East 21–0

"We wanted that #1 spot, and we knew in order to do that, we had to beat them. Going into this tournament we were expecting to win, and we accomplished that," Narit pointed out.

Jordan bookended the conversation: "To know we have the ability and the focus to beat a team that has the ability to make it to San Antonio feels great. To be recognized as one of the state's top teams is good, but this win was not enough for us to reach our main goal of getting to state. This is a great confidence boost heading into district."

After the victory over Stony Point, we earned the bragging rights and the bulletin-board material as the #1 ranked squad in the state. With a week off between games, Coach Wester adjusted the practice schedule to only shooting drills and light movement. Weekly weight-room workouts were moved onto the court with foam stretching afterwards to allow the players' legs to recuperate.

Assistant Coach Jamie Smith and I orchestrated an eight-station circuit with dumbbells, ropes, and heavy balls while Coach Godwin led the stretching. Coach Evans' JV players followed the varsity workout shortly after. It had been a long two months of six days a week with no let-up. The guys didn't say much, but a few members were showing signs of stiffness and becoming worn down. Above all, they were just tired.

Everyone needed the rest. With school closed for the holiday break, the early practices and free afternoons and evenings provided family time and an opportunity not to think about basketball.

Coach Wester was more concerned with keeping the fellas together mentally as well as physically, as district competition resumed at home with crosstown rival Plano Senior on January 5.

Two seasons ago, we entered this same game 20–1, the lone loss at the hands of Wolfforth Frenship High, a community just southwest of Lubbock, in the finals of the Cedar Hill Tournament. Plano Senior, our crosstown rival, entered the contest then with an unblemished 20–0 record, nationally and state-ranked #5.

Plano beat us like we stole something. The Wildcats, physically bigger and athletically better, also maintained an emotional edge that was too much for us to overcome. The game was a learning curve for our staff and players. East had to commit to a better strength and conditioning program. Plano Senior finished that year with an outstanding 33–1 record, 14–0 district champions, but lost in the first round of the playoffs to a stubborn Lake Highlands squad.

Game 22 – Plano Senior vs. Plano East #1 @ Plano East

Our players didn't need much pushing or rah-rah for this game. The "been there, not allowing a repeat from two years ago" mentality echoed freshly in their minds but became a quick afterthought once the ball was tossed.

It was Jimmy King Night—East's most famous alum and summer ball coach—and in front of a packed house. Chairs were set out along the home court sideline for his family and teammates.

The play on the court went according to plan. East exploded out of the gate with a first quarter 22–14 margin. However, Ty Mason's offensive run kept Plano Senior close at the half: East 34, Plano 25.

Coach Wester made a minor defensive adjustment at halftime, and the point of emphasis allowed our defenders space off the cutter. We cruised in the second half with our half-court game, finishing 34–28. East pulled away from Plano for an impressive fifteen-point victory.

"Justin himself defeated us twice last year on buzzer beaters. I couldn't let him get into a rhythm," Xavier stated, who drew the defensive responsibility on Buenaventura.

"There are teams you just have to beat. Plano is that team," Brew later told a reporter.

Plano East 68 – Plano Senior 53
Plano: Mason 27 pts, Buenaventura 9 pts, Jones 8 pts

DJ 22 pts, 9 reb, Jordan 15 pts, 8 reb, Isaiah 10 pts, Rachard 8 pts
East 22–0, District 3–0

Many a team's season has come to an end with a single player's injury. We had been fortunate thus far, with little to no setbacks in this area, and to this point, had not lost a player for any length of time due to a major injury. But the following Saturday practice, as we were preparing for Coppell, we had our first of several brushes with season-changing experiences.

Xavier suffered a bruised thumb at McKinney Boyd and was held out of the Rockwall game, but during our routine alley drill—a competitive one-on-one challenge—Isaiah, guarding Rachard, caught an elbow to the nose. I was on the baseline and witnessed the entire sequence. They collided, and Isaiah went to the ground. I rushed over to him and instantly saw the pool of blood puddling under his face.

In an instant, the alley drill kept going, but everything else stopped.

I shouted to Coach Godwin, "Go get Foley!"—our athletic trainer for basketball, who was in the training room. I walked toward Isaiah and handed him a towel to wipe his face. Isaiah rose to his feet and sprinted to the restroom in the front lobby of McAfee Gymnasium to get a perspective of the damage.

The energy in the gym shifted from competitive to cautious. Because this wasn't just about the injury. It was about watching one of our players—the team captain, an inspiring member who lived for this opportunity—possibly being lost for a long stretch, just when everything was falling into place.

Coach Wester motioned the guys to the other end of the basketball court and followed Isaiah and me to the lobby.

"My nose is broke; my nose is broken. Is it broken, Coach?" Isaiah asked.

"I don't know. Wipe your face so I can check it out. Don't hold your head back; you might choke," I responded.

I wasn't a doctor or trainer, but I'd suffered a few broken noses before. *It is broken,* I said to myself. "Let's go see Coach Foley." We exited the gym restroom for the training area.

Foley inspected the nose and cheek, then calmly asked for Isaiah's parent information. I had already made that call to Mrs. Brewington while in the restroom, and she was one step ahead of us from that moment on.

It was later confirmed that Isaiah's nose was broken. The question now was: how long would Isaiah be out? And more importantly, how would the team respond to losing one of their team captains?

Coaches always preached the "next man up" mentality, but who really trusted this coaching point? We did. Over the past three seasons, we had lost a key member or two for short periods with the flu, an ankle injury, or other happenstance, and our response was always the same: get as many players ready to play as needed. *Hard work pays off.* This was another reason for carrying fourteen guys on a squad. Enough to have two teams for scrimmaging during practice, plus a few extra for injury or other circumstances that could keep a member off the court.

There were several guys who could assume the starting point guard position with Isaiah out—seniors Narit, Rachard, or Ethan—all three capable and expected to do a good job. The players were mismatched on teams every day for practice, allowing for better competition and putting guys in game-like situations where coaches could put the best players on the floor at any moment. Substitutions would change and role responsibilities be altered, but with very little drop-off in production.

Game 23 – Coppell High vs. Plano East #1 UIL, #1 GASO, #2 MaxPreps @ Plano East

East defended well in the first stanza, taking a 21–14 lead and outscoring Coppell 36–23 at the midpoint, but we weren't playing sharp. Coppell kept the game within reason with timely shooting and evened the score 35–35 in the second half. East continued with another double-digit margin of victory—our nineteenth in twenty-three games this season.

East had four players with double-digit scoring, and two were one rebound away from a double-double (DJ and Narit). Narit, earning his second start, adjusted to playing point—not an easy task—and shot 12/13 from the charity stripe.

Coppell 58 – Plano East 71

Coppell: Lapsiwala 22 pts, Fleming 13 pts, Macken 12 pts

DJ 18 pts, 9 reb, Narit 17 pts, 9 reb, Jon 13 pts, 5 reb, Jordan 11 pts, 7 reb

East 23–0, District 4–0

Game 24 – Plano East vs. Plano West @ Plano West

East made their second crosstown trip in 10 days, this time against the other rival, the Plano West Wolves. The Panthers displayed a shooting exhibition, scoring almost half a century at the break, 44–27. East played all fourteen team members, with nine scoring in double figures.

Isaiah returned but with an assistant—a plastic mask to protect his nose and facial area. The mask, however, lasted only about one quarter before he abandoned it and placed it in his travel bag. "I couldn't see a dang thing. It caused my visibility to be off, and my teammates teased me," Isaiah said.

We did suffer a minor injury: senior shooting guard Ethan bruised his right thumb during warmups. The bruise didn't factor much in the game, as Ethan hit 4/7 from beyond the arc for 12 points, though the thumb was noticeably swollen at the 8 a.m. practice the next morning. Seniors Rachard (11 points on 3/9 from distance) and Xavier (7 assists) helped direct the Panthers on the evening.

Plano East 88 – Plano West 61
Plano West: Wilcox 22 pts, Rolle 8 pts, Walton 8 pts, Cravens 6 pts, Lavu 6 pts
Narit 17 pts, 7 reb, DJ 16 pts, Ethan 12 pts, Rachard 11 pts, Jordan 11 pts
East 24–0, District 5–0

Game 25 – Hebron High vs. Plano East @ Plano East

District game #1 and a rematch from the Frisco Mavs Tournament in early November, which we had taken control of late in the third period for a double-digit victory. If anyone had doubts about the Panthers' mental approach to the second game of the trifecta, they were extinguished after the first period.

A red-hot East squad jumped out with a commanding 19–7 lead and bookended the fourth quarter 23–16. Hebron closed the margin to 15 late in the third but lost in a rout. Things were coming together beautifully in our basketball circle.

Plano East 68 – Hebron High 43
Hebron: Haynes 18 pts, Jenkins 8 pts, Brenning 6 pts
DJ 16 pts, 6 reb, Jordan 11 pts, 8 reb, Narit 6 pts, 12 reb
East 25–0, District 6–0

Game 26 – Plano East vs. Flower Mound High @ Flower Mound

Flower Mound High, the final game in the first round of district play, brought back deep feelings for Wester and me. Memories that stirred resentment and anger, but also fueled the fire.

Eight years ago, on a cold Friday night, East and Flower Mound were in a heated race for the fourth and final playoff spot in District 6A, Region 1. With two games remaining, Plano West and Lewisville had qualified, and four teams—Flower Mound, East, FM Marcus, and Hebron—were battling in head-to-head matchups that last week. A little magic was needed if East was to earn a position.

As anticipated, a tightly contested atmosphere was true to form. Shortly after the ball was tossed, activity in the Flower Mound student section erupted, and the East spectators caught a glimpse of the ongoings.

The cheerleaders, who brought signs for the game, began matching words with the cheers. Whether on purpose or not, the words held high spelled *White Power.* This occurred multiple times throughout the first period and again in the third. To add to their prompting, several members of the current baseball team painted their faces and bodies in black paint.

Many East fans and the junior varsity players took offense. A few verbally confronted the students and addressed the administrator on duty, but little to nothing was done until halftime. Prior to the break, varsity assistant and Head JV Coach, Jason Hall, left the bench to further explore the ruckus and calm his players. The signs were eventually confiscated. But shortly thereafter, the verbal abuse—non-basketball related—along with slurs and other comments, began to be hurled at the players.

However, with all the commotion and unrest in the stands, a pretty good basketball game was taking place on the court. Flower Mound was fighting off an East rally, holding a two-point lead with 0.9 seconds remaining on the clock and fifty feet for a game-winner or tying basket to send the game to an extra period.

About midway through the third period, an East player suffered an ankle injury and needed assistance from under the basket. Close to the Flower Mound student section, I could hear students making racial slurs and jungle sounds toward our injured player. I motioned to and walked over to speak with the administrator in charge, but she only shrugged her shoulders in response.

There is no place for this kind of activity in high school sporting events, but we see it or read about similar occurrences daily, according to social media. Not here. Not to one of my players. But the situation became even more personal as the next sequence involved my son, Chauncey, a junior point guard at East in 2014–2015.

Coach Clarkson, then the Head Coach for East, called our final timeout and drew up a playground play on the clipboard. With the team closely standing, shoulder to shoulder, the five guys called upon to execute the design communicated their duties. Coach Wester and I looked at each other, puzzled somewhat by the play drawn and slightly more concerned about whom the play was for—Chauncey.

Our best free throw shooters available were Isaac, Chris, and Devin, in that order, but the play design used them as decoys, with Devin, having the strongest arm, as the inbounder.

The design was for Devin to fake a long pass to either player at mid-court, giving Chauncey time to set a screen on the baseline. After the fake throw attempt, Devin, being left-handed, was to sprint to his left, drawing defensive attention. The defender, using his high energy to deflect or block the ball, would chase after Devin and run directly into the screener, Chauncey.

Honestly, I didn't think the call would work. Surely, Coach Littleton advised his player to be smart and not commit a violation. *This play? No way it works.*

The referee handed Devin the ball, blew his whistle, and began the counting motion when—another whistle sounded. "Bleep, bleep, bleep." Two players were on the ground.

Coach Clarkson's play worked to perfection. Chauncey was knocked to the ground. A foul was called. A thunderous gym was now quieted as the players walked the length of the floor for the possible game-tying free throw attempt.

Players on our bench jumped with excitement, hugging and high-fiving one another, while the home crowd sneered as a round of boos echoed, vibrating off the arena walls.

As a coach, I was delayed in my reaction, attempting to demonstrate cool and collected emotions, already thinking about the next move. But as a father, one can become a victim of the moment. I was walking with Chauncey every step of the way, yet I was fifteen feet away, sitting locked arm-in-arm with the coaches and his teammates.

Meanwhile, this was what he had practiced every day for the last five years: the chance to give his team new life, an opportunity to put everything he had worked so hard for on the line. It can be overwhelming—downright devastating to the conscience and fragile ego—if you aren't successful.

Those thoughts, millions of others, bombard the brain all at once but must be as fleeting as Usain Bolt's 200-meter dash. Chauncey's daily ritual was to make 10 consecutive free throws before leaving the gym. His sacrifice to the East family.

The student body was louder and more raucous than ever on the first attempt. Most of his teammates didn't watch, burying their faces in their hands. *Swish.* String music. Chauncey and every East supporter gasped for air as the ball hit the net.

A momentary sigh of relief flowed through the visiting bench. The home sideline watched with the same intensity, hoping for a different outcome. Coach Littleton motioned his counter play as Chauncey received the ball from the referee, performed his routine, and released with perfect rotation. *Shrrp*—nothing but net.

A pin dropping on cotton could be heard as the free throw silenced the crowd, ending regulation at 56–56 and forcing overtime.

Flower Mound would surge ahead and win this controversial thriller 75–73 in triple overtime.

Bringing even more attention and awareness to the matter, the story garnered national attention on *Good Morning America*, *NBC Today*, and local ABC affiliate sportscaster Dale Hansen, a legend in the sports world, who spotlighted the game on his weekly Sunday night commentary *Unplugged*.

To top off the evening, Coach Wester—our designated bus driver—took an extra-long time to retrieve the bus. Coach Clarkson ran out of things to say to the team, and the loss somewhat eliminated us from postseason contention. But there was a method behind Coach Wester's tardiness. He found our ride home had been entered and vandalized—reeking with defecation and urination throughout the yellow dog. "It took me about 25 minutes to clean and make it tolerable for the ride back to campus," Coach Wester remembered.

Coach called me and asked me to meet him outside the gym driveway. As I exited, he explained the situation. *You could smell the odor before entering the bus.* I re-entered the gym, found Coach Littleton storing chairs, and shared the information. Littleton apologized and contacted his AD, Principal, and Superintendent.

Truth be told, the bus stunk to high heaven. We rode with multiple windows down, and it was a frosty night.

We—Wester and I—have had an instant dislike for this matchup ever since.

The game tonight with Flower Mound was over before it began. Coach Wester shared his memory of coming to Flower Mound, and I shared mine. Either could be fuel enough, but being greeted with boos from elementary students gathered to sing the National Anthem only reinforced it. Their current student body was equally as rude as eight years prior.

With approximately 14 minutes before tipoff, during warmups, I stopped our players and ordered them to punish the Flower Mound players for the things the fans were shouting at them. Absolutely despicable and disrespectful. Again, adults and staff were present, and nothing was done to correct the behavior.

After the first period, the score was 28–4, and their fans were chanting "overrated" at our team, calling them out by their government names, making slanted-eye gestures, and other choice sounds. Our fellas played through the taunts and almost held the Jags to a school-low 23 points. East had five players in double figures, and twelve of the fourteen participants scored.

Plano East 74 – Flower Mound 23
FMHS: Gummakonda 7 pts, Burkhalter 4 pts, Cargo 3 pts, Muller 3 pts, Jacobsen 3 pts
Jordan 12 pts, 7 reb, Narit 11 pts, 8 reb, DJ 10 pts, Xavier 10 pts, Jon 10 pts
East 26–0, District 7–0

End of the First Round of District Play.

PLANO EAST VS FLOWERMOUND

ALUMNI NIGHT

FINAL REGULAR SEASON GAME

WHITE OUT GAME
FEBRUARY 13, 2024
7:00 PM AT EAST

"Everyone must choose one of two pains: The pain of DISCIPLINE or the pain of REGRET."

- Jim Rohn

Chapter X

Ka Boom (District 2nd Round)

Game 27 East vs Flower Mound Marcus @ Marcus High

Round two of district is always tougher, having once played and with game film to make the necessary adjustments or improvements. Detailed preparation and a walkthrough session is utilized before the team boards the bus for the hour shuttle. Each player should be familiar with their role and focused accordingly with the game plan. Marcus gave us a challenge last ball game with their ability to shoot the long ball.

Returning from a long six-hour ride and championship win in Arkansas, the guys didn't remember that this team can shoot it well, and the half-a-day turnaround before a tough district opponent required much discipline, which we didn't demonstrate. No surprises this time.

A relatively packed gymnasium welcomed the Panthers in shootaround during the junior varsity halftime break. The jeering from the nonpartisan crowd appeared to inspire the guys. Ethan,

155

Xavier, and Izan composed an impromptu dunk contest with several attempts of 180-degree reverse windmill and one-handed, off-the-backboard tomahawk slams against the rim, ricocheting to mid-court.

It seemed to me that they were relaxed and in game mode. They got in a good sweat before reporting to the locker room for more pregame ceremonies of foam rolling, jump rope, stretching, and going through the scouting report.

Something our program picked up from the volleyballers was traveling with music. Coach Wester purchased a speaker for our basketball program with the intention of learning how to practice with and through chaos and distractions when they present themselves. Now, we bring our own distraction, blasting the sound system on the bus ride and even louder when entering our opponent's sanctuary.

This time, both teams, the junior varsity and varsity, strolled into the gym with Drake's "God's Plan" blaring loudly in the foyer, drawing an eerie stare from the Marcus fans and family members.

The atmosphere in the locker room did not mellow, and the enthusiasm amped up with Xavier's playlist assisting the tone the players wanted to unleash on the Marauders. As I finished with the player assignment, Coach Wester delivered the knockout pep talk with, "Play like a state champion would play."

The tip was as close as Marcus would be all evening.

A tremendous man-to-man defensive effort stymied the Marcus shooting from behind the arc to 23%, making 6 of 26 attempts. The Panthers took a commanding lead at the half, 44–17. On the night, East made the same 6 of 14 from distance and dominated the paint area for a massive 30-point road triumph over another state-ranked district foe. The eleventh victory by 25 points or more.

Plano East 77 - Flower Mound Marcus 47
FM Marcus: Susko 16 pts, Harris 8 pts, Comett 6 pts, Robinson 6 pts, Ramnanan 5 pts.
DJ 15 pts, 9 rbds, Jordan 15 pts, 8 rbds, Narit 10 pts, Isaiah 11 pts, Xavier 7 pts.
East 27–0, District 8–0

Game 28 Lewisville vs East @ Plano East

SENIOR NIGHT

It is customary to celebrate Senior Night on the last home game of the season. This event presents a myriad of distractions for everyone involved. A different set of emotions and preparedness, outside of the basketball world, infiltrates the functionality of basketball two hours before the ball is tossed. The booster club members take charge as the coaching staff concentrates on all things basketball.

For the eleven players, the three managers, and three trainers, this is their basketball version of utopia. Isaiah and Jon are four-year members on the varsity; six have three years—Rachard, Jordan, Ethan, Xavier. Two years for Narit, Seth, and Chima, and first-year members Ammani and Carter. Team managers Gabby, Kaylee, KJ, and trainers Kinsley, Shirley, and Gabriela are first-year members as well. Along with their parents, they became overwhelmed and excited to participate in the evening celebration.

The contribution from our managers and trainers is invaluable in the everyday existence of East basketball, and the booster club's decision to recognize their importance to the program is admirable. As customary, each mother is presented with a red or yellow rose, and likewise for our female managers and trainers. Shortly afterward, family and group photos are taken, making a memorable evening for all involved.

In addition to the excitement on the date, Archie McAfee Gymnasium received an upgrade with the lighting system over the summer break. The lighting, antiquated at best, is now easily accessible from the hallway, no longer a trek to the locked PE closet located in the south end of the building.

The new features can be manipulated or adjusted instantly, from bright to dim without being turned completely off. No waiting time to cool down or warm up. High beam or low, whatever is desired. As soon as Godwin and I were made aware of the functionality, plans for how and when to test the new lighting equipment took flight. We envisioned and wanted to create an atmosphere that would ignite and amplify the Jungle, our Eastside student cheering section, hopefully increasing their rowdiness.

Senior Night was designated on the schedule for the unveiling. With the excitement of two top-ranked teams, a Friday game, and the purposeful intention of energizing the student body to new heights, it provided an intimidating atmosphere for almost any opponent. But for the Lewisville Farmers, this was the show.

I inquired with our theater teacher about our stage lights on campus—if so, was it possible for basketball to use them at home games? And would our theatre students be willing to join the fray and cheer on their #1-ranked classmates? The remembrance came from the Flower Mound Marcus championship seasons when, as district opponents, they made three consecutive state championship appearances in Austin, winning back-to-back in 2011–2012.

Their theatre department shared in the enthusiasm while utilizing the spotlights during the player introductions and pregame ceremonies. Becky and I saw a smaller brand while shopping at a local hardware store, so I asked our booster club president, Mrs. Chotikavanic, to purchase four reasonably priced fog lights for our home game presentations.

During seventh period, our practice time, the City of Plano Fire Marshal, with two of his assistants, met with our Associate Principal, Rob Eppler, to inspect the facility due to the anticipated crowd expectancy. A lot of people coming and going, in and out—not exactly what anyone wants to be dealing with on game day.

Our program, if memory serves right, has hosted many big games during my tenure as an assistant: 2002 Dallas Lincoln, with future NBA player Chris Bosh and their #1 state and national ranking visited. In 2006, DeSoto participated in our three-team preseason scrimmage on campus; they were #1 ranked in Texas. Flower Mound Marcus, in 2011 and 2012, was ranked #1 in both the state and nationally, featuring future NBA player Marcus Smart, Phil Forte, and Nick Banyard.

The last team was Plano West, in 2015, entering McAfee ranked #1 in Texas and bringing four Division 1 athletes to the table: DJ Hogg, Mickey Mitchell, Tyler Davis, and SoSo Jamabo.

There had been some huge crowds, some close to being fully packed and several slightly over-capacitated draws. But NEVER has an East ball club been ranked #1 and hosted a top-ten opponent. In any sport, at any time, ever.

"This is awesome, baby, with a capital A," to borrow a phrase from ESPN sportscaster Dick Vitale.

Last, to tie a bow on the distractions, our DJ for tonight's game showed up toward the end of walkthrough to set up his equipment. Coach Wester chose to stop fighting situations, called a halt to walkthrough, and gave last-minute instructions about what time to report back to McAfee, then dismissed the guys. Chick-fil-A, the team's favorite gathering place in Murphy, Texas, was chosen for their meal. Meanwhile, Godwin was mopping the floor, Smith and I were pulling out the stands, setting up the scorer's table and chairs, and Coach Evans' junior varsity players tended to the rails and balls before retreating to the locker room to dress.

Coach Wester headed down to the weight room—his space before home games.

On the other hand, the music was under the microscope of Mr. "J Cruz," who has orchestrated the musical portion of our program the last two seasons. This week's rotation selection of local emcees—the infusion of live tunes for the audience's enjoyment— has separated Plano East's veejaying from every other gym in the area. "J Cruz," father of Ammani and a member of K104's *Dee Dee in the Morning* crew, a local radio show in Dallas, highlighted Plano East. The awareness ushered in a large amount of publicity to and from the DFW metroplex, making claims that Plano East is the place to be for great high school basketball.

The live entertainment addition brought a wholly different fervor, an eagerness, and a frenzy to the game. It was the extra—and extra was needed. Our booster parents' purchase would assist in the experiment, constructing an unforgettable environment for the senior class. Something that could further hype the audience was paramount for an evening of success. In preparation for this event, several junior varsity players attempted to practice the lighting several times, but all attempts failed. However, Coach Godwin's decision to go on with the pregame entertainment was heady and surprisingly rare. "The light show expectations could push the enthusiasm in the gym over the top," Coach Evans whispered.

Coach Williams, Defensive Coordinator and bookkeeper for the home games, played the theme of *Darth Vader* for the visiting team as their introductory rendition—just a bland afterthought for the moment. As Coach Williams finished with the visiting head coach, the musical guest began to spin our theme song for the game, *Mystikal, Here I Go.* With the instrumental start and a slight crescendo, like a mixtape, the beat matched the energy of the student section.

Simultaneously, the gymnasium went totally pitch black and a gasp fell over the crowd.

With McAfee on edge, Athletic Director and Head Football Coach Anthony Benedetto took the microphone, and his energetic exuberance set the stage. Performing his best Michael Buffer rendition of the renowned boxing public announcer, he shouted:

"Everybody, get on your feet! Take your phone out and turn on the camera light. Stand up, everyone, get on your feet, and let's hear it for your #1 ranked Plano East starters!"

A scene which many on social media would one day rival in references and receive mentions as one of the best high school basketball introductions ever in the state of Texas.

With all the pregame commotion and shenanigans, the on-the-floor activities were spectacular, as envisioned. Both teams played at a breakneck, action pace with big shot after big shot, great individual moves, and the intensity of a playoff climate. No fear detected. Only a district championship and state bragging rights at stake. A normal Friday night game anywhere in America—and the pageantry presentation did not disappoint.

In front of a capacity crowd, the Farmers and Panthers battled to a 14–17 first quarter before East forged to a 9-point halftime advantage, 31–22. Lewisville took control in the third behind an inspired defensive pressure attack, causing multiple miscues and resulting in easy buckets. "We're fine. Take care of the ball," Wester said during the timeout.

Wester called a play designed for an overload, looking to get a size advantage or a mismatch inside for an easy counter to their trapping. After several ball reversals, Jon saw the angle and tossed a nice entry pass to DJ for the lay-in, halting the Lewisville run and ending the period with an 18–12 stretch, cutting East's deficit to three, 43–40.

During the break before the final period, both teams gathered around their respective coaches, wiped off, took some hydration, and anxiously awaited instructions. The referees conferred at the scorer's table, then positioned themselves to start the last stanza.

Time for big-time players to make big-time plays.

I am not superstitious, and I don't believe in luck. There is no such thing as luck—only preparation taking over opportunity. Repetition until it becomes a reality. Doing something over and over and over until it becomes a normal, natural action or reaction. Then a vision is formed, and when that formation is practiced, expectations occur.

Next is the opportunity.

After Lewisville tied the game at 43–43, DJ scored with a nice spin move from the free-throw line elbow for the kiss off the glass. Xavier took over, scoring the next six points on two layups and one monstrous, jaw-dropping posterization. Completing his first in-game dunk off a dribble handoff from DJ—right down Broadway— he sent the crowd and our student section (the Jungle) into a roaring frenzy.

"I had told Jeremiah, a fellow student photographer, that I was gonna come from the right to the middle and dunk it. I saw the lane. Just took off. I rose up," Xavier later claimed.

The dunk was unexpected and spontaneous at the same time, but Lewisville managed to battle back yet again. After a missed free throw and a Coach Martin timeout, the Farmers' best player AJ received the inbound pass at the volleyball mark, took a quick dribble to his left, positioned himself for a great look at the rim, and launched his Hail Mary opportunity to tie the game at 62 with the last-second shot of regulation.

The entire gymnasium was on pins and needles, hushed while the ball was in flight. However, the shot ricocheted off the side rim.

This was tremendous theatre.

Lewisville 59 - Plano East 62
LHS: McPeters 18 pts, Chambers 17 pts, Brown 11 pts, Crawford

10 pts.

East: Xavier 16 pts, DJ 15 pts, Jordan 11 pts, Isaiah 9 pts, Jon 8 pts.

East 28–0, District 9–0

Game 29 Plano East vs Plano Senior @ Plano

Cross-town nemesis, East ventured across Central Expressway to visit Plano Senior. In rivalry games, quite often, records are thrown out the window and emotions can become heightened with both teams. The game is a virtual toss-up if not handled correctly. We know who the better team is, and our preparation is top priority.

Plano's Chin offense, a version of the Princeton tree, requires communication and discipline. If their post player is allowed to set good screens, it will spell problems for us attempting to slow down the back cuts and open shooting. Our guys must be dialed in.

"The losses to them last year make me sick to think about," Jordan is overheard saying. "We gave them two wins," Isaiah replies.

There is little banter on the ride over to Plano. Roughly seven miles to the west provides the latest challenge, and the guys watch video clips, read through the scouting report, and mentally replay the first game matchup.

A good attendance is expected as our fans are beginning to buy in and travel to away games. This will almost be a home game, so to speak—more of the black and gold than maroon and white.

For the most part, Plano Senior played as well as predicted, defending their home court. But a slow first and third quarter allowed us to maintain a comfortable lead behind balanced shooting of 7/13 from distance and 22/26 from the charity stripe. The six-point hole in the opening period was the closest the Wildcats could muster on the evening.

Plano East 61 - Plano Senior 50
PSHS: Mason 24 pts, Hampton 9 pts, Buenaventura 7 pts.
DJ 17 pts, 12 rbds, Narit 11 pts, Jordan 9 pts, Jon 9 pts, Isaiah 7 pts, Rachard 6 pts.
East 29–0, District 10–0

Game 30 Plano East vs Coppell @ Coppell

Friday, February 2nd, the local weather forecast called for an overcast, cloudy evening commute with light to heavy rain in some areas of the DFW metroplex.

After a short shootaround, the varsity and junior varsity players and coaches loaded the bus for the 30-minute trip. Meanwhile, Assistant Coach Jamie Smith and I gathered the bags, the team managers, trainers, and boarded the Special Education minibus, which was recently purchased at the beginning of the school year.

After driving the older van—dirty and needing a paint job in the worst of ways—on several road games earlier in the season, I asked Head Principal David Jones and Special Education Coordinator Anthony Ruttenburg for permission to use the new campus minibus. Two meetings were established, and after discussing the details for usage, bus overcrowding, and bus coverage, Principal Jones granted permission.

Throughout the afternoon, the rain came down in sheets, sometimes harder than usual, but on Coach Wester's command, both bus and minibus pulled out of the parking lot for Coppell as the bell rang ending the final class of the day.

The blessing was that Coach Smith drew the driving assignment because I was negligent with the scorebook, roster sheet, and scouting report. The ride would allow me time to get all these needs done, and I could eat and enjoy my Chick-fil-A pregame meal. However, the real blessing was Coach Smith's calm demeanor and even quicker reaction as a combination of events took place.

While following the team bus traveling west on the President George Bush Freeway to Coppell High, the rain began to fall more heavily and cars whistled by as if we were racing at Texas Motor

Speedway, when a loud BOOM was heard. Instantly, bags, water bottles, food, and such went flying as we realized our minibus was airborne.

Coach Smith, being alert and unwavering in this crisis, responded with racing-school training like none other. He steadied the vehicle while manipulating the same-way traffic driver—avoiding driving off the freeway onto the North Dallas Tollway commuters—about a 40-foot drop, before coming to a halt on the shoulder.

What took only seconds seemed like years flashing in my mind.

Unbeknownst to us on the minibus, a few of the players, including Coach Wester through his rearview mirror, had full view and witnessed the entire incident.

After pulling over, Coach Smith and I checked on KJ, Gabby (managers), and Tiffany (trainer) as we exited the bus to take a quick look at the damaged vehicle sitting on the side of the road. I phoned Coach Godwin, and he acknowledged they were aware and would circle back for us at the Midway Rd./Rosemeade Pkwy roundabout.

While waiting for the bus, I then called the bus barn to report the accident, gave specific details of the vehicle's location, and my observable main damage walkthrough.

It took the bus approximately 15 minutes to retrieve the five of us and put the arrival time at Coppell about 20 minutes behind schedule. Coach Godwin phoned the Coppell coaching staff to keep them apprised of our situation and possible arrival time.

Coach Smith saved us today. "I'm quite sure if I would have been behind the wheel, the outcome may have had a different ending." To God be the glory.

A solemn feeling hovered over the remainder of the bus ride to Coppell High, but the near fatality did not affect the energetic evening that was forthcoming. As the junior varsity players were rushed off the bus due to our tardiness, the varsity musical adventure began as we entered the gym with Xavier's choice leading the way. I was somewhat rattled, still, and it took a while before I returned to normal. There was a game to be played, and the best way to give praise and thanks was to perform to the best of your abilities.

Thankful was the mood of the day. It was chilly outside, rainy, and as many as five on this trip were absolutely blessed to be here— to be healthy and alive.

With all of the excitement and chaos, I forgot that I invited an old, old friend to join us for the game tonight. Coach Mike Anderson, former head basketball coach at UAB, Missouri, Arkansas, and recently St. John's University, had relocated to the area to rejuvenate and visit with his daughter.

As the spectators and fans entered the arena, many of our parents hurried to make their way to Coach Smith, the lady managers, and myself, quizzing us about the incident and offering condolences for the tire blowout on the way to the game. The word of mouth regarding the accident spread like the flu and added to the interest in the game attendance. People flock to near-tragic situations, and some in attendance came to see if it would affect the team's performance. It did not.

East's defensive presence again set the tone for the game, holding every Coppell player that played to 8 points or less. A 41–20 halftime was followed with a 35–31 second-half tilt. The Panthers had four score in double figures, a team total of 10 assists, 10 steals, and 30 rebounds. Xavier's confidence was soaring as he had 3 monster dunks, and Izan demonstrated his jumping ability with an even nastier rim-shaker.

Plano East 77 - Coppell 50

Coppell: Macken 8 pts, Pehl 6 pts, Socks 6 pts.

DJ 15 pts, 8 rbds, Xavier 15 pts, 3 dfl, 2 stls, Rachard 14 pts, Jon 10 pts, Jordan 8 pts.

East 30–0, District 11–0

Game 31 Plano West vs Plano East @ East

Not ever being in this position—undefeated and knowing that with the remaining games on the schedule we are heavily favored—is new. I coached a Little League baseball team to an almost perfect regular season but lost the second-to-last game on a walk-off hit. We went on to win the city and regionals but lost in the state qualifier. That is the closest I've gotten to a perfect season as a coach.

As a player, I was fortunate to be a member of multiple undefeated city championship ball clubs in my youth, but nothing after the fifth grade. This run the boys are on is special in every way possible. It is our duty not to mess it up, derail, or allow outside forces to corrupt the current streak. Not envy or jealousy among the players or coaching staff. No egos. We must work more diligently to keep our circle small as the playoffs approach.

Within the coach's office, our discussion turns to what to practice and one game at a time. Every thought is geared to becoming the best Panther I can become today. Becoming a better player, a better teammate, a student, and a friend. This journey is a special journey, and only a few teams have ever accomplished an undefeated season capped with a state championship. Not in 20 years and not in the top classification. This is doable.

There is a tsunami of confidence developing in the East locker room, but that energy needs to stay focused and humble. Hard work has provided this program and this specific group of players an avenue and vision to do just that. There is no fear of winning, but if not of the same mindset, the fear of losing can creep in.

Today it's us vs. West. Nothing more, nothing less.

The Wolves are outmatched, outclassed, and overwhelmed. East dominates the box score and those plays that don't go into the box score but win games. Examples like deflections, backside help on defense, and altering shots are what make the team flow. The unselfishness, the extra pass, and trusting in your teammate to do his job.

Our packed student section, the Jungle, serves as judge and jury. They harassed the West ball club from the beginning of the JV game until the last whistle of varsity. The Panthers take a convincing 18–10 first quarter with a swarming defense, crippling West's young backcourt. A 15–11 second is managed, but East's 31–15 third spells doom for West. In consecutive games, Rachard scores in double figures, and Ethan hits a three, but his defensive presence and rebounding are impressive.

For the twentieth time on the season, every East squad man to dress out plays, and twelve of the fourteen score.

Plano West 58 - Plano East 77

West: Lavu 19 pts, Rolle 10 pts, Cravens 8 pts.

Jordan 17 pts, 6 rbds, DJ 14 pts, 8 rbds, Rachard 11 pts, Xavier 8 pts, Jon 8 pts.

East 31–0, District 12–0

Game 32 Plano East vs Hebron @ Hebron

The trifecta—a third bite at the Panthers' apple—is the Hebron Hawks' mindset and a possible upset if we are overlooking them. But the guys are confident and appear relaxed, as demonstrated when they lined up for air layups with the ball rack locked while the Hebron players exited the competition gym to watch the junior varsity game next door.

A season ago, Xavier, Carter, or Rachard—our best antagonists, who would've verbally addressed our opponents to no end—instead laughed off the act and chose to mask the exercise creatively until the assistant coach returned to the area with two basketballs.

Isaiah and Narit didn't appreciate the gesture, and it became a topic of conversation during the pregame warm-up as both teams entered the court. The tone was set.

Hebron, 21–9 overall and 8–4 in District, fighting for a playoff position, took the first quarter 15–13. East kept our composure and matched the Hawks' intensity with a 17–12 second and a 30–27 halftime lead. Coach Wester equally managed his nerves, praised effort, and demanded more aggressive play on defense. "The tougher team will win this game." But the message wasn't about physical toughness—it was mental. Execution, execution, execution was key. No mistakes would be the difference.

Considering what was at stake—an undefeated season, including the district championship—the locker room was calm and encouraging. No raised voices. No thrown dry erasers or broken clipboards today. Only water and towels for the most sweated. A highly contested battle was occurring before our eyes.

After an even 11–11 third period, which unveiled some interestingly intense moments, Isaiah and Jon answered with a triple apiece. A strong defensive fourth quarter, behind several key deflections by Jordan for transition buckets, established the 8-point margin for the victory.

Plano East 63 - Hebron 55
Hebron: Haynes 15 pts, Mennsfield 11 pts, Moore 11 pts, Massingale 8 pts.
Jon 20 pts, DJ 16 pts, 10 rbds, Jordan 11 pts.

"Always remember that leadership is a privilege. When you're in a leadership role, your influence may affect the trajectories of people's entire careers [and, often, their Lives!]."

Chapter XI

ALUMNI Night

Without question, there is absolutely nothing more important to a coach than the relationship developed with and amongst his players, me included. This night has grown over the past decade and, to a large extent, every former player from both programs—the boys and girls—are invited back for a magical evening of rekindling friendships, telling war stories, and enjoying a great basketball season-ending event.

Due to our success and wanting to reward this senior class with the best final home game experience, an open invite was sent out one week prior through social media, text, and word of mouth to all interested former Plano East alums. The only request was to RSVP Coach Godwin or me by noon on game day.

The preparation turned out to be a bigger undertaking than anyone could have possibly imagined. With the three major television networks clamoring for campus exclusivity (ABC, CBS, NBC) and our local photographers—professional and students— seeking interviews with Coach Wester and players, time was sensitive: the Fire Marshal restraints, police coverage, the game itself was a release.

Up to 75 alumni RSVP'd, with individuals and families flying in from as far west as California to some from the East Coast of New Jersey. Others drove from Tennessee, Kansas, and Arizona. In-state alums from Houston, San Antonio, and El Paso inquired about tickets, seating, and what functions would be held before and after the game. The biggest surprise was the number of people who arrived before the school day ended to walk around the campus and revisit old memories.

A small group of former players attended the pregame walkthrough—the '85–'86 and '93–'94 classes to be exact—and asked for a tour of the old locker room and to take pictures. Following the walkthrough, the junior varsity members, with the custodial staff, retrieved approximately 80 chairs from the cafeteria as Coach Godwin and Coach Smith directed the setup.

Many visited the campus before arranging for an early dinner or meeting up with teammates to return later for the game, while some sat in the stands and watched the JV.

The format was very similar to that of Senior Night, including priority seating with some chairs in front of the home crowd, a live disc jockey providing the musical entertainment, and a next-level player introduction. But never, in school history, had a Plano East program hosted such an event while ranked as the #1 team in the state.

A two-page pass list was typed out and delivered to both ticket gatekeepers—another adjustment credited to the newfound enthusiasm generated from the season's success. And not only with an undefeated season on the line, but the surreal possibility of tying the school record of 33 wins in a given season made this a monumental achievement.

During warmups, several local celebrities and former NBA, NFL, and baseball players were seen among the fans in the stands. Tony Hill, a former Dallas Cowboy and East dad with his son Anthony—the former four-year letterman, three-year starting point guard, and a member of the 2008 Regional Finals team—walked over to greet me under the basket for a brief handshake and hug.

The OGs of Plano East basketball, for their attendance, were rewarded with floor seating, a hot dog, and a drink, while the current players met, greeted, and played for the players who built this tradition.

"This is a beautiful thing to witness, and a long time coming. I thought to myself, appreciate the moment. Take it all in and breathe." I did both.

A great evening was unfolding as the clock wound down to tipoff.

Thank you again, Waxahachie, for the vision.

Game 33 Flower Mound High vs Plano East @ East

McAfee Gymnasium was standing-room-only as both teams reported to the floor. Each exit door was manned with two Plano Police, Collin County Sheriffs, or a combination. All seven East administrators, the Golden Girls dance team, and cheerleaders joined a packed house full of fans and spectators from the area, wanting to get a glimpse of the Panthers in the last regular season home game.

In the locker room before the game, seniors Narit, Jordan, and Isaiah decided to add an only-player chant they would say as they finished warmups before heading to the bench prior to player introductions.

The squad kept their circle tight and recited: "Who got my back? I got your back. Who got your back? I got your back."

Another reaffirmation of their team commitment.

The game wasn't much more than a practice session, beginning with an 8–2 run, followed by a Jordan takeaway, transition layup, and the foul for Narit. DJ's bucket and an assist to Ethan gave the Panthers a 17–7 early lead. A third offensive rebound and putback by Jordan with a pair of threes—Rachard and Narit—the rout was on. Moustafa's mid-court steal and slam dunk with 2:34 in the second quarter put East up 37–14.

East continued in the second half in the same fashion it began—with great defense, holding Flower Mound to a team-low 29 points and sharing the ball for easy baskets—while scoring a season-high 95 points. Every player suited up played a minimum of nine minutes, and eleven scored, capping off a 66-point regular season win.

Highlights included Ethan's unexpected two-handed slam dunk in traffic. He also shot 3/6 from distance to lead the Panthers in scoring. Carter had 5 rebounds, 3 assists, and twice attempted dunks (0–3 on the year), but his effort and personality kept our team's energy elevated. And without question, Athletic Director/Head Coach Benedetto's bedazzling playoff shirt stole the show.

Flower Mound 29 - Plano East 95
FM: Gummakonda 8 pts, Jacobson 6 pts.
Ethan 17 pts, Qazi 15 pts, Narit 11 pts, DJ 11 pts.
East 33–0, District 14–0

With the win, the team tied our program's most hallowed school record of total victories with 33 and became district champions for the second consecutive season at 14–0. Shortly after, the players thanked the family and friends for their support of Eastside basketball. The ladder was brought out to finish the celebration.

The net-cutting ceremony is an important tradition performed after a major basketball feat has been accomplished. But this wasn't the net we were looking to cut down. The fellas had a more devious activity on their minds: a Gatorade cooler shower for Coach Wester. They began plotting at halftime, and after the dousing, the team took to diving on the wet court to conclude the evening.

We were the No. 1 team in Texas and #2 in the nation, according to MaxPreps.

The celebration—priceless.

In *The Book of Basketball* by award-winning sports columnist and podcaster Bill Simmons, he once interviewed Isiah Thomas, the two-time NBA champion point guard and Hall of Famer for the Detroit Pistons. He asked what is the "real secret of success," and Thomas summed it up in one word: chemistry.

Isiah Thomas didn't cite talent, skill set, or toughness—all needed ingredients to make a run for a title. Instead, he credited his teammates' ability to sacrifice their individual goals for team achievements. "On any given night, you couldn't tell who the best player or the leading scorer would be," said Thomas.

This is the same fate and philosophy our Panther squad has taken to task.

"The Bond That Links Your True Family Is Not One Of Blood But Of Respect And Joy In Each Other."

- Richard Bach

Chapter XII

Fish Day

My pops, Allie Sr., was a country boy. Raised in McGregor, a small central Texas farming community located 15 miles west of Waco, Sr., known as a jack of all trades, became a carpenter, college graduate, army veteran, barber, high school football coach, and a principal for 35 years. He worked hard with and for the community he served, but his passion, first and foremost, was fishing.

Every weekend Sr. could be seen in the early dawn of the day, loading up his green Buick LeSabre with fishing gear, eager to accept the challenges of Mother Nature from a bankside nearby. This was his oasis.

If memory serves me correctly, Sr. longed for the 3–4 hours of sitting in the shade, waiting on any of the river monsters to tug on his line. Bass, crappie, or perch—but his favorite was catfish. And Sr. was the old-school fisherman. No fancy equipment, rod and reels, no. He was a cane pole man. On the side of our house were seven or eight cane poles varying in length from 14–17 feet.

Sr. would also dress for the part, wearing yellow or green one-piece jumpsuits and a straw hat. He was proud of his country bumpkin appearance all the way to the cane pole holders fastened to the passenger-side doorframe. I looked forward to our fishing excursions. His passion became my passion.

Wednesday, the day after our last regular season game, the district coaches met for the season award and accolades nominations. Coach Wester scheduled a short shootaround and a rehab check-in for the injured players and asked me if I wanted to take the boys fishing, to organize a bonding activity on our campus pond.

The answer was heck yes; I could use the relaxation and have fun teaching the basic fishing norms. For several of the players, this may have been their first experience fishing, and who knows, a great first impression could lead to a lifetime of memories. Coach Godwin and I frequently fish with our P.E. and special education classes in the spring. The fishing rods and reels were purchased by our previous P.E. director from Wal-Mart: 10 Zebco and 10 Abu Garcia, 2 tackle boxes, 10 spools of 10–20 lb. Trilene fish line, and a 6-foot fish net.

After our coaches' meeting, Coach Smith and I began pulling the equipment from the physical education closet, checking for workability, and putting hooks and sinkers on each rod and reel.

During my lunch break, I drove over to Lavon Lake Bait and Tackle to purchase live bait—minnows, worms, and whole kernel corn. Worst case scenario, corn attracts every kind of fish, ducks, and turtles around the pond.

When the guys entered the locker room area, they knew instantly what the day had in store. Some seemed surprised, and most eyes gleamed with excitement. A majority of the team had never been fishing, and they could barely contain themselves. It was like going to the amusement park—running over to get in line first, grabbing for a rod and reel, jumping up and shouting. An amusement park adventure, to say the least.

Everyone was handed their own fishing pole, and we exited the locker room, a few walking while others rushed toward the ponds on the other end of campus. Coach Smith and I walked, towing all the bait, our fishing poles, and the tackle box in the wagon. Coach Richardson, Plano East Lady Panthers coach, joined the fun after his school day was concluded.

To see their eagerness and smiles of anticipation is what being a part of a team is all about.

Once we arrived on the bridge, a quick lesson on how to cast the rod and reel was provided, as well as how to bait the hook. Both lessons carried an inherent fear that comes with every fishing adventure—getting hooked by oneself or another. My only request was for everyone to stand 20 feet apart to prevent such an accident.

It was a beautiful day to go fishing and an even better day to share, hang out, and spend meaningful, purposeful time together. In the past, we either went to a movie, went bowling, or to a teammate's residence for dinner, but a fishing outing had been on my mind for several years.

The East basketball fishing outing was a smashing hit. A slam dunk. Two hours of fun, laughing and joking, catching small bass, perch, and catfish. At the end of the day, only a few lines were broken and a couple of bigger fish wiggled themselves off the hook, but no one was injured or needed to see a doctor. Not everyone experienced catching a fish; however, a fun day was encountered.

Carter caught the biggest fish. Rachard and DJ caught the smallest. Ethan managed to pull in a small bass, while Moustafa missed the most but landed a nice-sized bass before we left the ponds for the evening.

1st Round Play-Offs
Bi-District

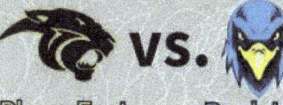

Plano East   VS.   Rock Hill

Monday, February 19th
Tip-Off @ 6:00 Pm
Hebron High School

"Consistency Wins.

Because it's not what you do once in a while that matters, It's what you do every day that counts."

@bechampionminded

Chapter XIII

4th Quarter (The Drive for State)

A great playoff run has been the ultimate driving force since that February 24th, almost one year ago to the date, defeat at the hands of Lake Highlands in the second round. Since the CBI tournament in late December, Coach Wester organized a rehab regimen to follow the weightlifting maintenance on Wednesdays and Saturdays. The rehabbing and leg recovery are the key ingredients for not tiring in the most important time of the season.

An old-school treatment procedure is the whirlpool ice bath (for 3–5 minutes) to pull away the lactic acid buildup from the wear and tear of long practices or games, and foam rolling with band stretching to assist in muscle recovery by reducing inflammation and soreness.

Utilizing these methods of rehab to preserve their legs and harness their energy, along with spending as much time together as possible, aids in our team bonding activities as well.

The state tournament consists of a three-week fantasia of basketball whiplash. Seven single-elimination games divided into four statewide regions with 128 teams total, each feverishly competing for the right to be the state representative at the Alamodome in San Antonio, Texas.

Could this be destiny? Fate?

Who knows, but there's something oddly poetic about our team. Three years building, developing a trust of team chemistry, summer camps, and a plethora of game-time experiences. Several local coaching staffs texted and made a request of Coach Wester: "Can we attend one of your practices or workouts?" They wanted to see what we do and how our players respond. "What's your magic potion?"

In a nutshell: personal sacrifice and chemistry.

Can you coach unselfishness? How is it taught to give up a very good shot for an even greater one? The inclination to dive for loose balls or to take a charge? "Our players won't do such things," one coach shared.

The guests, however, found no magic pill. No verbal expression that was unique or earth-shaking. Only hard work and trust. A desire to do what other players or teams are unwilling to sacrifice, the art of making plays that don't show up in the stat sheet but exemplify the total buy-in and what separates the good from the greats.

Following the weight room session in the indoor facility, the Saturday before the first-round Bi-District game, I shared a baseball reference with the guys to help them focus. We had a few baseballers, Isaiah and Rachard, and they understood this simple scene. In the movie *For the Love of the Game*, actor Kevin Costner's character, the pitcher "Chapel," while dealing with outside issues, had allowed them to spill onto the mound and was recently having problems hitting his spots.

While positioning for the next batter, the crowd noise became louder, particularly the man along the first base dugout shouting negativity in his direction, when Chapel reminded himself to take a step or two back, breathe, and "Clear the Mechanism." His method of refocusing, eliminating the chatter.

Our best preparation for the playoffs is to remove all distractions not basketball-related and embrace the challenges ahead. As Jon states, "Get locked in."

Prosper Rock Hill, coached by Shawn Williams—a star player for the 2007 State Champion Duncanville High, whose career I've seen grow over the years—was first on our tour of seven stops.

The game-day routine for playoff games provides a more intense atmosphere and offers anxieties to the time-regimented, chaotic day. For the common fan, they go to work or school, then show up for the game excitingly energized to cheer for their team. Parents and booster clubs coordinate t-shirt sales, carpools, paint signs, etc., while coaches themselves prepare the team managers, jerseys, video equipment and bags, the clipboards, dry erase markers, prepare the scorebook, scouting reports—gather together all the basic needs for any game-day ritual. But this isn't just any game day.

It's chaotic at best. Full of anticipatory themes and anxieties. But that's what the playoff environment encapsulates: an opportunity for greatness. "The guys have to play at a different level. If they maintain their composure, keep our turnovers to a minimum, and limit the mental mistakes, the rest will take care of itself. We have to raise the bar, and I think they will. This team can focus. They can really, really focus. If they could have focused last season, we would have gone further. We weren't ready, and God works according to His timetable."

Coach Wester and our athletic directors negotiated a Monday evening game. Although it was an off day for our students (no classes), the goal was to keep a normal regular tournament schedule day for our players and create stress for our opponent, who had a full day of school activities on their schedule.

Schedule:
2:00 – Team Lunch at Chipotle
3:00–4:00 – Practice at East

4:15 – Depart Plano East to Hebron High

5:00–5:30 – Practice at Hebron

6:00 – Tip-off

The 11-mile ride to Hebron High, the chosen arena for the contest, was smooth and seamless. Familiarity had its place; however, the stakes were somewhat higher than the previous visit. The gym was as quiet as a church mouse when the officials greeted us at the front door and guided the players to the locker room for the evening. But I set our musical playlist in motion on the bus ride, and it continued until we exited our scheduled practice time of 5:30 on the floor. The perks of being the visiting team—and we were wearing our new gold jerseys.

Controlled aggressiveness embodied with self-confidence and a single goal in mind had 30 minutes to redistribute their emotions as Rock Hill had the court and eager patrons began to line up outside the arena doors.

Once the pregame warmup began, I utilized the expanded minutes to work out my own anxieties, thoughts, and size up the opponents by getting in steps walking around the court. First, walking 10,000 steps daily—that's approximately 5 miles or equivalent to 8 kilometers—was requested from my doctor and is easier on the body compared to lifting weights.

Secondly, I could get an up-close look at the players—their length, height, foot movement—and report it back to our coaches for adjustments or tweaks.

Finally, I briefly greeted the reporter and radio host before I took a view of the family and friends congregating in the stands. I shook hands with former players and parents showing their support, and then sought hugs from my immediate family: wife Rebecca, daughter Quinae, sons Da'Ray and Chauncey, and grandchildren Kaiden, Karter, and Kinsley. This was the best of the best—a mini reunion.

I was now in a good, clear space for competition.

Game 34 Round 1, Bi-District Plano East vs Prosper Rock Hill @ Hebron High

There was high energy in the air as the attendance for the state #1 ranked team, along with the Panthers faithful who travel well, filled the gym just moments prior to the opening tip.

A lively crowd watched as East scored easily and often, but Rock Hill fought back to a 19–10 first quarter. In the second period, the Panthers' defense tightened even more, holding the Hawks to half of their first-quarter output—5 points—and to a total of 15 at the break, giving the Panthers a commanding lead, 34–15.

A 32-point avalanche in the third blew the game wide open, and the Panthers finished with a decisive 37-point Bi-District victory in Round 1. Isaiah had an outstanding shooting performance from the three-point line and led our team as five Panthers scored in double figures off a team total of 20 assists. Xavier added a thunderous dunk from a Jordan rebound—quick outlet to DJ at midcourt for a one-dribble, assist statement. "We comin'."

Isaiah had a great shooting night, sinking five three-pointers on his way to being our leading scorer with 16 points, but he was responsible for 27 total by adding 4 assists and 7 rebounds.

After the final horn, the guys momentarily jumped into each other's arms, then quickly lined up to show sportsmanship with the Rock Hill players and Head Coach Shawn Williams, who was a star member of the Duncanville 2006–2007 undefeated 5A State Championship team at 39–0. Shortly afterward, the players made a mad dash toward our student section, located in the north end of the gym, to high-five and thank their friends for coming out to support—a tradition Coach Wester began a couple of years back.

Immediately following the student celebration, the team gathered at center court for the Bi-District trophy, a gold ball meticulously designed to symbolize the acknowledgement of capturing the first phase of hopefully seven on this memorable journey. The circle concluded with their latest chant. They began to sway and… Narit said…

"Who's got my back? I got your back. Who's got my back? I got your back. You got my back? I got your back."

Along with tonight's win, these Panthers became the winningest team in school history. To celebrate the victory, the team voted for dinner at Velvet Tacos in West Plano.

Plano East 88 - Prosper Rock Hill 51

PRH: Milton 19 pts, Garcia 14 pts, Hutchinson 8 pts.

Isaiah 16 pts, 7 rbds, 4 asst; Jordan 15 pts; DJ 12 pts; Jon 11 pts; Narit 11 pts.

East 34–0, Bi-District Champions

Game 35 Round 2 Area, Plano East vs Highland Park @ Coppell High

A Friday night, 7:00 pm game against a team we played earlier in the season, a third time in the last year, and with a respected coaching staff, Head Coach David Piehler, could be problematic. They were the most physical ball club we had played. "They play disciplined, fundamental basketball and run good stuff," the scouting reports read. Our coaches had borrowed a set or two from them, and we knew this would be a battle.

Unlike the previous playoff game, the atmosphere in the Coppell arena was low, even with the later start time that gave travelers time for an early dinner before the game. With the extra day of preparation, one would anticipate an equal-sized crowd with doubled excitement because of the history between the programs.

Schedule:
3:30–4:15 – Shootaround/Walkthrough
4:20 – Depart for Coppell
5:30–6:00 – Practice at Coppell
7:00 – Tip-off

The last time we made this trip to Coppell High, a mishap—a blowout—occurred on President George Bush Freeway. But not today. Everything ran as smooth as spring water flowing downhill.

During our team shootaround, I could sense the players' focus was good. The execution of sets was flawless, and their attention to detail was on point. In the locker room, the stretching and attitude were ordinary, and our routine approach hadn't deviated by any means. Nonetheless, the aura felt slightly indifferent.

We returned to the court for pregame at 6:42, 18 minutes before the scheduled tip, and our energy appeared drained. I began my walk around the court, getting steps in and sizing up the opponents. "We aren't making shots," I mentioned to Coach Wester. As I continued my step-seeking ritual, I saw college teammate Nate White of Connect Dallas behind our bench. Nate has been a consistent supporter over the years.

To add to the distraction, about three or four Highlanders, dressed in movie-character garb, under our basketball goal, continuously shouted "overrated" and "you suck" at the players. The young men bordered on obnoxious, and while some of their rants became corny, they were effective.

My second go-round and Coach said, "Change it." I gave another shooting exercise, seeking better results. "Motion offense." The double-action layup progression proved to be the necessary station for the shot-making they needed. Just seeing the ball go through the net is brilliance to the faint of heart.

The Highlanders outplayed us in the first quarter, leading 12–11. They were again the more physical team and made some timely shots. But after two quick timeouts from Coach Wester, our defense took over and clamped down on the Highland Park shooters, holding them to 6 points in the second quarter. A pair of deep bombs from Rachard sparked a 12–2 run late for a 30–18 halftime upper hand.

Coach Wester didn't say much at halftime. He questioned us assistants about what we were seeing from the sidelines before calling the team together. "Keep defending hard. Go get some shots up," Coach Wester said. He was short and fuming.

An almost even third quarter, won with a 15–13 margin, and the Panthers' aggressive brand of defense opened a 15-point difference, 29–14 in the fourth quarter, providing the Panthers a 29-point blowout and the Area Championship. Rachard went 3 of 4 from the three-point line, but as a team, we shot 5/16.

Our defense defended at a high level, collecting 15 steals and 9 deflections, resulting in 19 turnovers for 18 transition points. Highland Park shot 50% from behind the arc but could only attempt one free throw in the game. It was also Isaiah and Jon 100th victory as varsity players.

Coming in second place on the night was having four of the five head principals to lead Plano East in attendance: Mr. McAfee, Plano East's first campus principal from 1981–2004; Mrs. McDonald, 2011–2014; Mr. King, 2014–2023; and Mr. Jones, a Plano East alum, 2023–present.

Mr. McAfee briefly visited the winning locker room, and I introduced our school's inaugural principal—the man who coined our warmup shirt phrase, "Winning with Class," which is also found in the halls and classrooms around East campus—to our players.

However, after the end-game celebrations, the acceptance of the Area gold ball trophy, the running to the student section, circling for the chant at center court, and after Mr. McAfee's visit in the locker room, Coach Wester addressed the players as if the game was a loss.

The message sent, loud and clear, was that if this effort and attention to detail mirrored tonight's performance, it could be our final game of the year. The next opponent—most likely Allen—was a far superior ball club, from top to bottom, and we would lose if things weren't corrected.

Team dinner after tonight's game was at a reliable quick fix: Whataburger. An early practice was scheduled tomorrow morning for scouting and film breakdown of Allen.

Plano East 74 - Highland Park 45
HPHS: Beckett 16 pts, Stribling 10 pts, Ariyo 5 pts.
DJ 15 pts, Narit 15 pts, Rachard 13 pts, Xavier 7 pts.
East 35–0, Area Champions

Game 36 Round 3, Regional Quarterfinals
Plano East vs Allen @ Garland Curtis Culwell

Tuesday, February 27, 2024—game day—was a normal day in every sense of the word, except it wasn't normal. It was Round 3 of the playoffs versus our nemesis, Allen High. There was quite a buzz of excitement in the air around campus like none felt in 30 years, and the players were enjoying the attention.

We had played Allen earlier in the season—Game 1, to be exact, in the Cowtown Tip-Off at North Crowley—and we put in as much film work as possible, which allowed us to procure a special game plan for them. We had the best coaching staff in terms of breaking down an opposing team's tendencies, and if they didn't make adjustments, they would be in trouble. That was first.

Secondly, our players weren't afraid of the Allen Eagles—it was almost the antipode. This was a crosstown rivalry, literally five miles up the road with a substantial, passionate history. We knew their players and coaches, likewise, but as a team, the Panthers did not fear Allen.

Preparation leads to opportunity. Mentally, the film work is done. Physically, everyone is healthy and rested. Emotionally, their confidence is present and growing. They know they have the answers to this test.

Then the modicum of luck is posited, but there is no such thing as luck. Luck is that preparation meeting an opportunity.

This group of players and coaching staff has been preparing for such an opportunity the last three seasons. The past 43 years. No luck involved. Repetition upon repetition. Execution to confidence. Confidence to belief. Belief to trust. All equaling success.

People don't see the foundation being built beneath the surface. Success isn't just about what is visible; it's also about the unseen roots of being disciplined, resilient, and the experience from preparation. Because one doesn't see the progress doesn't mean it isn't taking place. The strongest tree doesn't grow overnight.

Curtis Culwell Center, the site chosen for the Regional Quarterfinal game, is no stranger to us at East. The neighboring multipurpose facility, under Executive Director John Wilborn, has always welcomed the presence of Plano and is located on the Garland–Richardson boundary of President George Bush Freeway, approximately 7 miles, or a 10-minute drive. It is the perfect locality and accessible for a potentially large attendance. Curtis Culwell's seating capacity is 6,800, and with standing or suites availability, 8,500. Hence, a home-court advantage is forthcoming.

If my memory serves me right, I was a witness in the stands for the Seagoville, LaMarcus Aldridge years, the South Oak Cliff "Slim Shady" Darrell Arthur and Kevin Rogers four-year run, and, more recently, the Plano West vs. Richardson Berkner in 2014. Not so long ago, East enjoyed participating in the Garland ISD tournament, played in the championship game on a few occasions, but never in front of a capacity crowd. Tonight's contest could be record-setting for high school basketball attendance in this facility.

The fellas called for blackout attire from the Panthers faithful and requested to don the new gold jerseys with the black long-sleeve warm-up shirt that sports "Winning with Class" on the front for the third consecutive outing.

The Itinerary:
3:35–4:15 - Regular practice at East
4:25–4:45 - Travel to Curtis Culwell Center
5:00–5:30 - Shootaround
5:30–6:00 - Locker room
6:00 - Doors open
7:00 - Tip-off

Lady Panthers Head Basketball Coach, nephew Derrick Richardson, escorts the team as our bus driver for tonight's game and good conversation along the way, whose team recently finished a playoff run themselves.

The ride to Curtis Culwell is short but productive. The players read over the scouting report:
Allen High starting lineup vs. Hebron High #'s 1, 3, 4, 15, 24.
Key Players: #1 Trent, 6'0" jr; #3 Nehemiah, 5'6" soph; #15 Deandre, 6'7" jr; #4 Kaiden, 6'3" sr; and #0 Aric, 6'2" sr.

Game Notes on Defense: Will trap ball screens. Very aggressive on defense, handsy. Jump every pass. Will leave a man open to help or create pressure. Gets into foul trouble easily. Make hustle plays. Will show pressure, then fall back to man. Rebounds well. **Game Notes on Offense:** Everyone touches the ball. They want to get out and RUN the entire game. Shoot a lot of bad shots. They are easily sped up and chaotic.

And watched several video clips on their phones. The most important thing they do is relax and enjoy the musical collaboration of Xavier's aux. Nothing too hard or rambunctious, but something to their liking to set the mood for the competition they were expecting to face for the couple of hours.

As the Culwell opens its doors at 6:00 pm, the fans, like ants, impatiently scurried toward the available seating—first come, first served. East directed to the south section of the arena and Allen to the north. Each patron eagerly anticipating a battle of wills to unfold before the evening's conclusion.

There is a lot of energy floating about, with two highly animated squads ready to duel. Much trash is being said through social media, but the airwaves aren't where the game will be played. An expectant capacity crowd could appear, and it may be the largest thus far, with the nation's #3 and state #1 team vs. the #10-ranked clubs squaring off in Garland.

Meanwhile, in the locker room, Coach Wester shares his vision of the game with the players before taking the floor, "I don't believe that coaching will come into play much. It is going to be a fast-paced game, without a ton of adjustments. Just big-time players making big-time, game-winning plays."

Speaking things into existence.

"Now, in this game, what does a game-winning play look like?" And the guys verbally share their responsibilities: rebounding/blocking out our opponents. Rebounding, rebounding, rebounding, and getting those loose 50–50 balls. "If you do these two things, I can't IMAGINE we don't win this game. I've taken lots of tests, and I don't remember being this prepared for them. You know what they do! You know what we do. How much of your life have you spent preparing for the chance to play in a playoff game between the 6A two biggest schools in the state of Texas? A ton of times, hours upon hours upon hours, you have prepared for this game. It's finally here. Play as hard as you can." Coach Wester's last directive.

1–2–3 Eastside, 4–5–6 State Champs… and with 20 minutes showing on the wall clock, the Panthers exit the locker room for the pregame warmup.

Our Eastside enthusiasm immediately overtakes the arena as the first group of fans to enter the seating begins to shout out that familiar East chant… "PLANO, PLANO, EAST, EAST. PLANO, PLANO, EAST, EAST," as other bystanders also chimed in unison. Louder and louder, until it seemed as if anyone and everyone was here to support the Panthers.

The next indication of symbolism came about after our starting lineup introduction: the East fans, in a mandated blackout attire, turned their backs during the Allen players' introduction. A huge, massive sea dressed in all black turning away is the visual, and it was intimidating.

East begins the game with a 6–0 run, 9–2 after a Jordan three, and settles the tightly contested first quarter with the five-point lead, 13–8. A Jon three-pointer followed by reserves—Rachard taking a charge and Ethan draining his second three-pointer of the quarter in transition—causes the baffled Eagles' head coach, Clark Cipoletta, to call his second timeout in the quarter. The Panthers' active hands on defense and spacing the floor off turnovers spark a 20-point second quarter, giving the Panthers a commanding 33–17 at intermission.

No matter the crowd noise or how close the game appears, we hold a double-digit lead over a dangerous Eagles' squad for three quarters of the game.

Allen manages a 21–17 third-quarter advantage, but Xavier explodes and scores 9 points for the Panthers after going scoreless in the first half. He finishes with 17, all in the second half, on the evening as East dominates the last stanza 29–14, winning in blowout fashion. Adding to the mix is DJ's 17, with Jordan's 14 and Rachard's 11 points, respectively—East by 27.

The Panthers' defense, once again, was suffocating, holding a potent Eagles offense to 28% field-goal shooting while winning the transition and turnover battle. Our fan base is a major difference maker.

Plano East 79 - Allen High 52
AHS: Pane 17 pts, Thomas 11 pts, Myers 10 pts.
DJ 17 pts, 13 rbds; Xavier 17 pts; Jordan 14 pts, 12 rbds; Rachard 11 pts, 4 asst, 2 stls.
East 36–0, Regional Quarterfinals Champions

The team celebration continues with a sit-down dinner at Cheddar's.

Word is, tonight's attendance reports that over 4,000 tickets were purchased, and this is one of the biggest in Curtis Culwell Center history for a basketball event.

We are headed to Regionals, Friday and Saturday, in Fort Worth, Texas. This will be our first time to advance to the Region I tournament site—our fourth Regionals appearance; the last came in 2012–2013 in Region II at Midway High in Waco, Texas.

Due to NCAA-sanctioned rules in 2011, Baylor University and the NCAA and its member institutions are prohibited from hosting nonscholastic basketball practices or competitions, including tournament play, to eliminate the perceived notions of recruiting advantages for college programs that host these events. Plano East has previously played at the Wilkerson–Greines facility during the Coca-Cola Fort Worth Invitational at Christmas from 2005–2008.

The story that bears the truth: regionals have been the kryptonite to East's Superman. That unclimbable, monster hill of programs in our pathway to basketball nirvana. Prevailing thoughts are that if we can conquer a regional championship against the best of North Texas, our chances versus the other regional representatives are substantially greater to capture our first state title.

As a program, East has qualified four times for the Regional Tournament but only advanced to the state tournament once.

- **1993–1994:** 33–4, Region II, State Finalist
- **1999–2000:** 27–9, Region II, Semifinalist
- **2007–2008:** 30–6, Region II, Finalist
- **2012–2013:** 30–7, Region II, Semifinalist

I was fortunate to be on staff for East's last two regional appearances, and both times we left with that punched-to-the-gut feeling after suffering one of the craziest endings of an East basketball game in school history.

After rallying from a 15-point deficit in the first half, Coach Bleadorn, our head coach in 2007–2008, changed defenses from man-to-man to the 2–3 zone, and Houston Klein Forest went stone cold from the field, only scoring on made free throws. A pair of three-pointers and a steal from Diggs tied the game late in the fourth period.

A questionable five-second whistle gave Forest the ball with under a minute left in regulation. As if it transpired yesterday, the last few seconds still play in my mind today. The Forest point guard made a cross-court pass, which was tipped and caromed by an East player to a wide-open shooter in the corner, and nothing but the sound of the net was heard from the microphone under the rim.

Coach Bleadorn signaled for a timeout with 4.3 seconds remaining. Klein Forest up by 3.

With the length of the court to maneuver, Coach Bleadorn drew up a scaled play: Diggs, as the inbounder, ran the baseline from his left to the right. Smith and Uwaga screened for West, going left to right, while Hill cut under the double screen to the left. Diggs heaved an across-the-body football pass like Tony Romo to Terrell Owens—on the mark to Hill, who caught the ball in stride, and just like it was practiced every Monday and Thursday, Hill let it fly. From my vantage point, the ball looked true when it left Hill's fingertips.

Time sometimes erases details and hides circumstances, but the image of the ball in flight is burned into my memory forever. One inch to the left, the ball hits the square and banks in. One inch to the right, it's all net—we hear the same sound of the net previously from the Klein player. But no, the basketball gods blew the ball down, wedging it between the backboard and rim.

In a game of this magnitude, never before or since have I witnessed a game end in this manner. No words can describe the stomach-churning, nauseated feeling that followed. Utterly stunned, we exited the court bewildered. Sixteen hours earlier, our team had defeated the #4 ranked College Park Cavaliers, 62–42. This afternoon, we experienced the 1970s ABC's *Wide World of Sports* opening verse: "the thrill of victory and the agony of defeat."

The basketball gods owe the Panthers.

Regional Preparation

Wednesday practices with the players lately included the routine: one-hour shooting games for sharpness, a 20-minute weight circuit on the court, foam rolling and band stretching, and finishing with five minutes in the ice bath for rehab and recovery.

Thursday was a refresh and rhythm day. A back-to-normal practice on the court, with emphasis on preserving their legs and focusing on the mental aspects of the game. Very little contact, with no scrimmaging. Five vs. zero for execution, but shooting, shooting, and more shooting. In the meantime, our freshmen coaches broke down the scouting reports: one coach on V.R. Eaton, another on Keller High, and the third for district rival Lewisville.

Coach Wester delegated duties while he was bombarded with interview requests and head-coaching responsibilities. Coach Evans prepared and organized the itinerary for the Regional Tournament. Coach Godwin handled the scouting. Coach Smith had the exercise bag with the ropes, foam rollers, and towels. I was responsible for the jerseys, video equipment, boards, laptops, room assignments, and time management.

The boys had all their attention on the scrappy Eaton High from Northwest ISD, north of Ft. Worth. The second-place District 4 Eagles entered this matchup with a 26–8 record after defeating a tough Frenship squad in the Area Round, 57–54, behind veteran Head Coach Tim Thomas, who has accumulated over 600 wins, 10 Regionals appearances, and taken multiple programs to the state playoffs in his 26 years.

UIL 6A Regional Tournament Itinerary

Ft. Worth – Wilkerson-Greines Activity Center

Friday, March 1st

9:00 – Arrive at Plano East / Breakfast provided

10:00 – Depart PESH

1:00 – Practice at Wilkerson-Greines

2:15 – Depart Wilkerson-Greines / Lunch at Chipotle

3:30 – Arrive at Embassy Suites Downtown Ft. Worth

5:15 – Depart Embassy Suites for Wilkerson-Greines

6:00 – Arrival at Wilkerson-Greines / 1st Semifinal game in session (Keller vs. Lewisville)

8:00 – Tip-off vs. V.R. Eaton

9:30 – End of Game

10:00 – Board bus

10:30 – Arrive at Embassy Suites / Dinner (Domino's Pizza)

12:00 – Lights out

Saturday, March 2nd

8:30 – Wake-up / Breakfast

9:30 – Team meeting

10:00 – Clean rooms / Pack bags

11:00 – Depart Embassy Suites for Wilkerson-Greines

11:30 – Shootaround

12:30 – Locker room

1:00 – Tip-off vs. _____

2:30 – End of Game

3:30 – Board bus

4:00 – Dinner (Red Robin, BJ's, Jake's Burgers, Longhorn Steakhouse, Chili's)

6:30 – Arrive at PESH

Breakfast burritos and fresh fruit were provided by the booster club, and several mothers served the fellas at 8:30 am before heading to Ft. Worth later that afternoon. The boosters called for White-Out attire this weekend.

Around 9:05, that elevated feeling of adrenaline began to flow through my veins as I saw, from a far distance, a black AJL International Charter pull into the bus lane in front of Archie McAfee Gymnasium. A reaffirmation that our basketball program had reached the next level: the Sweet 16 round of the state tournament. The spoils of expected achievements.

A quick meet and greet with the bus driver, and I got first dibs on seating—the front seat across from the driver. After a look around, the managers, trainers, and coaches packed the bottom storage cabin with equipment before the players boarded. Officer Akin and Assistant Principal Abdelfattah organized and dropped off two huge boxes of snacks for the players before we departed the Plano East bus area.

However, today felt like an early preseason tournament travel day, not a lose-and-your-season-is-over day. Definitely not a state tournament vibe—but it was. And our players were extremely confident after blowing out rival Allen, the tenth-ranked team, by 27 points on Tuesday night. Today's opponent, Eaton, a squad from nearby Northwest that no one had heard much about, hadn't quite resonated on the fear spectrum.

A short haul (50-minute bus ride) began an elongated day. It was still a game yet a business trip all the same, and the guys didn't appear to be as attentive. But it was early.

Next stop: Wilkerson-Greines Activity Center, Ft. Worth, Texas.

Somewhere along the President George Bush Freeway, as the bus driver shifted into cruise control heading west, memories of the last East regional appearance instantaneously flooded my thoughts, and country singer Kenny Chesney's song *I Go Back* took over.

I cued the melody, and emotions once buried deep in my "never think about" box came rushing back as the lyrics pulled the remembrance of the last possession of the 2008 Region II semifinal game versus Klein Forest into real time. Then I reimagined the outcome. East wins, East wins, East wins, as the song concluded on my iPhone playlist.

The bus arrived about 20 minutes ahead of schedule to Wilkerson-Greines, and due to UIL shootaround rules, no one other than the team or coaches was allowed in the gymnasium during private practices. We had the 1:00 practice time, which gave us options: stay on the bus, get off the bus to stretch their legs, or allow them to walk over to the track stadium adjacent and across the parking lot to take in the track atmosphere. All chose to walk to the track together and take in the activities, passing time until we could enter the activity center.

During the practice session, a few of the players lost their normal intensity or focus: the execution and sharpness disappeared, causing Coach Wester to raise his voice—two times, to be exact—and change the flow with a circle-up at center court. Noticeably, something was off.

After the allotted time on the floor, everything was gathered, the ropes, foam bands, and we loaded the bus for lunch at Chipotle, then to the Embassy Suites Downtown Ft. Worth for check-in and relaxation.

Before you know it, a text from Coach Evans: "Bus departure at 5:15. Get all your personal game gear and shoes, downstairs in the lobby by 5:00." Everyone's phone beeps, buzzes, or clings in response to receiving the message except Chima's. I message the managers and Coach Foley, the trainers.

As accustomed, I hand the guys the scout report on Eaton as each enters the bus. Coach Wester emphasizes that Eaton is a good defensive, gritty ball club, but they have a difficult time scoring the ball. Their game falls in line with our philosophy: make it hard—harder—for them to score, and we score easy buckets with 4s or 5s (layups or paint touches, establish the inside presence). It will be only a matter of time before they wear down.

Our defense is becoming our calling card. We can press. We can apply good man-to-man pressure. We can take away any player and recover with backside help. We've challenged the guys to use their athleticism, to play angles, and to always stay between their man and the ball, creating deflections and turnovers.

The bus arrives at Wilkerson–Greines as the Lewisville/Keller game begins play, and a good crowd has already assembled. Eastside faithful also arrived early and cheer, "PLANO, PLANO, EAST, EAST," as we enter and take seats in the bottom section on the west end of the gym.

Again, the promise made during the spring workouts and throughout the summer program is being realized. When East enters a facility, "All Eyez on Me"—a Tupac Shakur reference—applies. The 6A #1 in the state of Texas, #2 nationally ranked Panthers have arrived, and that's what they wanted, worked so hard to achieve, and now have earned.

Smiles, handshakes, and chest pumps from the well-wishers and spectators are a lot—somewhat expected but premature. A game, still, has to be played, and this milieu is uncontrolled. The guys are told to sit, and the coaches deny all friends, family, and others from approaching or communicating with the team. At the halftime mark, we head to our respective locker room, as does Eaton.

Game 37 Round 4 Region I Semifinal Plano East vs. V.R. Eaton @ Ft. Worth, Texas

Maybe it was the new court, an unfamiliar gym. Or the excitement of playing in a regional semifinals game. Or simply being overconfident. But our guys went out a little sluggish. We had an early lead, 9–2, but mentally weren't clicking. We had several missed assignments that allowed the Eagles to manage a mini run, scoring six consecutive points to end the first period, trailing 19–8.

Honestly, Eaton brought the energy in the second and played to the best of their team's abilities, winning 10–7, keeping it close at intermission, 26–18, Plano East.

Not much was said in the locker room, but a re-emphasis on the defensive end and keeping in touch with our principles could put a bow on the contest. And that's precisely what the players did. After the halftime breather, the Panthers matched their opponent's energy and put a gigantic clamp on the Eagles, holding them to a seasonal—

and a Plano East playoff team—low of 2 points while boat-racing with 19 in output and without DJ, who injured his ankle earlier in the period. The Panthers ended the third stanza on a 13-point spurt to open a 25-point advantage, 45–20.

Eaton actually played hard in the fourth, 12–8, but it was far too little and much too late. East earned a 57–30 semifinal victory—the fifth consecutive, fourth double-digit playoff win—even when not playing up to their usual standards.

"But we knew it would be just a matter of time. It wasn't the best; we battle and wear teams down. We have to win in a different way and did today," Coach Godwin claims.

"I can't remember a game being so difficult, and we won by 27. Our guys appeared detached or distant most of shootaround, and that effort apparently carried over into the first half of the game. Our team's approach must be better tomorrow because Keller is going to be tougher."

Plano East 57 - Northwest V.R. Eaton 30
EHS: McCarthy 8 pts, Stokes 6 pts, Tarpeh 4 pts.
DJ 18 pts, 7 rbds; Jon 12 pts; Jordan 9 pts, 11 rbds; Rachard 6 pts; Isaiah 8 rbds.
East 37–0, Region I Semifinal Champions

10:00 – Board bus for Embassy Suites Downtown Ft. Worth

10:30 – Dinner / Domino's Pizza

11:00 – Players-only team meeting

12:00 – Lights out

Not knowing the status of DJ's ankle injury or his availability, as preached and practiced all season long, the next-man-up mentality is expected. Our team has been able to adjust and work through a few health situations along the way, but tomorrow's game will be the latest challenge for the Panthers if DJ isn't able to go.

The next morning, that Eaton hangover ten hours earlier rang hollow and was forgotten. During the morning breakfast, on a scale of one to ten, I'd say the mood is an eight. Relaxed, cool, and collected, a good night of rest is ample time for a fresh reset and the opportunity to compete on the biggest stage for the right to represent North Texas and Plano East for the second time in school history.

Xavier: "Last night, we had a players' meeting. We know that we didn't play our best; we played down to the competition, and we know we can't do this against Keller, or we will be going home."

Team meeting at 9:30 lasted approximately 30 minutes and only detailed the departing measures from the Embassy Suites and arrival for Wilkerson–Greines. Upon first glimpse, the guys looked as focused as ever. No laughing or joking. Dialed in. Apparently, the group meeting served its purpose.

While on many of our bus rides, the players individually listen to their own tunes and read through the scouting report. Today I noticed that no one had their earbuds or Beats on. So, I turned to the managers and asked them to turn on the speaker, connected the Bluetooth, and called on an old faith—Eminem—to set the tone to the gym.

The trip took half the time—12 minutes, or three songs—when the bus entered the parking lot. Coach Wester gave instructions, and to the side entrance everyone was escorted by the security officers into Locker Room C, same as yesterday.

Game 38 Region I Finals Plano East vs. Keller @ Wilkerson–Greines, Ft. Worth, Texas

This feels like a home game for the Keller Indians and their head coach, Zach Weir. Wilkerson–Greines Activity Center is only a 30-minute drive if you avoid tolls. They travel well and have great participation from their student body. The Indians will be making their second consecutive appearance in the Region I Finals—Coach Weir's third district title and fourth playoff in his fourth year since taking over the helm—and enter the Regional Finals game with a 30–5 record, #8 ranking by MaxPreps.

With two of the state's top-10 ball clubs battling for the Region I crown, a bigger-than-normal crowd is anticipated and expected. The Eastside travels very well, and the following has been increasingly growing with every victory.

Doors open at noon for the 1:00 pm tip, and as advertised, the gymnasium is bustling, and the intensity of the atmosphere fills the air. Unlike Curtis Culwell, the Area Championship gymnasium, the design of this building allows the acoustics of fans to get louder than the typical rabble; you hear everything, and there is not a bad seat in the facility.

In the pregame preparations, with Drake, Nicki, and Kendrick lowly playing in the background, the guys were getting locked in, attentive, and focused. Coach Wester writes the game plan on the board and states, "Keller is tremendous on offense but weak on the offensive glass. We have guys who can go get rebounds; this game could be over quickly. Get out in transition. They are way better in transition one way than the other— which way is that? Offensive. They don't get back on defense, and they have no answer for our inside game. If we do these two things, I have no doubt we come out as the winners."

DJ, who received treatments throughout the night and earlier this morning, huddles up next to me and communicates, "I'm 100% ready to go, Coach."

The lasting impression is that we couldn't afford to have a repeat performance from yesterday, or our perfect season would be abruptly concluded in the blink of an eye.

East exits the locker room first at 12:30 and Keller a few minutes later. Our players are laser-focused, making every shot, nailing each dunk with precision, and hitting on all cylinders. I begin our rotation shooting at the 12-minute mark and start my walking routine around the gym, getting my step numbers and sizing up our Keller opponents. I hear Levi, Coach Wester's oldest, calling my name. I motion to him to follow me as I open a gate in front of security, and Levi exits the stands onto the court. Whispering in his ear, "Go give your father a hug—he could use one," I continue my walk.

As I'm approaching Coach Wester, midcourt at the scorer's table and barking out "rotate" to our shooters, I mutter, "They aren't as tall as the scouting report says," and continue the walk.

Along my second walk around, I fist pump with a couple Keller players and greet their coaching staff, again barking commands to East shooters: "rotate." Then, stating to both Coach Wester and Coach Godwin, both on the logo center court, "DJ is moving around quite easily, better than I expected." I peer over the coaches' shoulders to the end of the scorer's table and notice Pete Nielsen, an old friend who's calling the radio broadcast for UIL today, setting up.

After a short hug and handshake, Pete bluntly asks the question: "How do you feel about the matchup?" My reply: "On edge, but God is kind. And honestly Pete, they don't have enough rocks in their pants." Then I continue my walk past.

On my final trip around the court, I notice Tom Inman, friend and former Plano Senior High and the 2005–2006 State Champion Head Coach, waving at me in the stands behind our bench. As well as my Arkansas teammate, Tony Ollison, and his wife Sherry, our college classmate and basketball coach, sitting next to my wife Rebecca, two of our four sons—Da'Ray and Chauncey, who's recruiting from his Texas A&M–Kingsville job—our daughter Quinae, with two of her children, Karter and Kinsley. Her third child, Kaiden, and her husband, son-in-law Jamie, are away for soccer. Seated on the next row is Coach Lambert and his wife Lisa. I gave and received acknowledgements to a few of my favorite people on hand for the afternoon competition.

The Panthers get off to a fast start, 11–0, with a dominating first quarter behind DJ's inside presence. At one point it was DJ 8, Keller 0. East up 22–13. The second quarter begins with Ethan knocking down a triple, his second of the game; however, Keller plays even with their point guards, Schank's 8–0 run and Guerra's 4-point play keeping the Indians close, winning the period 18–17. DJ responds, going on his second 8–0 run on an assist from Xavier, and East leads at the intermission, 39–31.

The score appears close, but the Indians—like I shared with Pete before the tip—didn't have enough rocks in their pants as DJ has his best performance of the season. Outscoring the Indians 20–19 in the third, DJ has 12 points in the quarter, his second 8–0 stint, and finishes with a season, game-high of 31. The defense clamps down in the fourth and ends the game on an 8–0 run, holding the talented, deep-ball-shooting Keller Indians to 10/29 from behind the arc.

Rachard, who's coming into his own, demonstrates why he is another difference maker on this team. Doing it on both ends of the floor and emotionally displaying to the crowd that the defender is too small to guard his 5'10" frame, he is a force off the bench who would be a starter anywhere else.

And he is correct. He is in a space that only a small group of players attain.

His drive-and-kick assist to Narit for a triple. Follows up with taking the charge on the next possession. Then spotting an uncovered DJ for a three-pointer, his second straight dime, and stealing the inbound pass for his dagger—a trey in front of the Keller bench. Rachard's only made bucket in the game. Four consecutive plays, and that effort turns the momentum back in the Panthers' favor, capping a 9–0 run to counter Keller's 4-point blast with 5 minutes remaining in the fourth quarter.

A 16-point win speaks volumes to the defensive effort the Panthers have been applying. They are accepting the coaching challenge while scoring with ease—music to a jovial Coach Wester's ear when that final buzzer sounds.

The long-awaited celebration springs into action. East qualifies for the state tournament for only the second time, and it's the 30th-year anniversary of the best team in school history. The victory lap around the Robert Hughes floor is fitting, and the circling up at center court to perform the latest team chant is not as moving as the customary cutting of the net. I ask the seniors to cut a piece and present the keepsake to Coach Lambert, standing at the wall of the stands.

No one deserved to be a part of this celebration more than Coach Lambert. And no one wanted this victory as much, is more loved or missed, than Coach Lambert.

It is an emotional event. One mountainous relief—the biggest pressure a person, coach, or community could muster—and the release that follows is not what I expected, most definitely not in that moment. Standing shoulder to shoulder with the players and coaches, I almost break down, but I hold it together until I hug Lambert. I shed a few more tears with my wife, our children, and grandchildren.

Standing in the gymway entrance outside Locker Room C, reflecting, Coach Godwin—off-beat as usual—begins to emphatically dance with and between the players, releasing some built-up emotions. Coach Evans seems even more delighted, if that were possible. Coach Wester suspects that, like Coach Smith and me, this team is getting better. Afterwards, we all simply enter the victorious locker room, where the lyrical sounds of Mystikal's *Here I Go* are boomingly blaring at top volume, and the dancing henceforth.

We have finally gotten over the hump, and it is humbling. It took twenty long years, and instantly—but respectfully—I need to acknowledge that many good coaches, better yet, great legends in Texas high school basketball laurels, haven't experienced what we will be experiencing next weekend. That realization should make one pause for a few seconds, to think and say, "WOW. We did this."

The locker room celebration lasts for approximately 30 minutes or longer, before security ushers a polite, "It's time to leave the building" grimace. The gesture is well received. The players gather their belongings, and everyone ecstatically loads the bus for Plano.

Coach Evans and Coach Godwin select Chili's Grill & Bar—a marvelous choice—as the victory restaurant for dinner. The directions are given to our bus driver, Mr. Harold: 15 minutes away, just off Interstate 20, in Grand Prairie, Texas.

The bus pulls into an empty Plano East campus about 6:25 p.m.

Three practices left and a lifetime of memories to gain.

Plano East 76 - Keller High 60

KHS: Schank 18 pts, Ramirez 15 pts, Fabian 10 pts.

DJ 31 pts, 6 rbds, 2 asst; Jordan 18 pts, 6 rbds, 4 asst; Narit 7 pts;

Ethan 6 pts.

Plano East 38–0, Region I Finals Champion

Over the last 36 hours, from all of the well-wishers through phone calls, text messages, and handshakes, Coach Wester has managed to juggle and distribute responsibilities among our staff while interviewing and fielding more requests than anyone could have ever dreamt.

So much so, our Plano ISD Communication Assistant Director himself will be escorting the local sports anchors from the Fox, ABC, and NBC affiliates to campus on Wednesday in preparation for the state tournament.

If anyone knows Coach Wester, distractions are the last thing he wants to be messing with—especially coaching in his first state tournament as head coach, being nationally ranked, and sporting an undefeated record. What else is on his plate? And naturally, several things happen to surface all at once.

Quietly kept and under the radar, *The Throne*, an up-and-coming high school national basketball tournament, from their president, chief operating director, and members on their selection committee, has been watching Plano East, Stony Point, and Beaumont United all season long, with the deep ambition to invite the next state champion of Texas into their field of 16-team tournament at the end of March.

However, never a discussion from the coaching staff or to the players on the possibility to play in New Jersey—but a parent's inquiry on the availability of their player is requested from Coach Wester. The only tournament on the minds of everyone is Lake Ridge, Friday night at 8:00 pm.

Apparently, the demands from the summer workouts, lifting all of those weights, the six-days-a-week practices, the daily competitions during skills, and doing the little things have their rewards.

From Eastside madness, UIL's official first day of scheduled practice for boys four months ago on November 1st—what seems like an eternity ago—everything comes down to the next three days of preparation, video watching, and finally, that often REM-dreamt trip to the Alamodome in San Antonio as a participant.

Monday: Practice

For practice, the schedule changes: meeting in Coach Wester's classroom for video first, then to the court for stretching, walk-through, and shooting.

This Lake Ridge ball club is more physical than skilled. They would much rather intimidate, push, and foul than play disciplined. Our ability to adjust and move the ball is key. The more the ball is rotated or passed, the more the defensive players have to move. Upon statistics, if the ball is rotated four or five times, the defense loses track of either the ball or his player's responsibility, making it easier for our game plan to work.

Defensively, paint presence, rebounding, and playing the passing lanes are our focus. Being the tougher team—both physically and mentally—maintaining our composure, with ball security and minimizing turnovers, is paramount. Then we need to raise the bar. Search for that intestinal fortitude and leave it all on the floor. No regrets. Go put on a show.

After a great practice, PESHPrints, Plano East's own award-winning journalism program, sends two student reporters to speak with several seniors and reflect on the team's journey for a feature story in the paper's next edition.

"Playing basketball at Plano East is unique. It's a brotherhood, and it's a bunch of dudes that have been playing together forever [four years]. We are all one mind," Senior Ammani states.

"We are happy it all paid off," Senior Carter reflects. "It's a big accomplishment [38–0], but it's not all about just basketball. It is more about what we've built as a team instead of playing just for myself."

Senior Iasiah: "What I've taken away from my last year is to treat every game like it's your last because you never know. I had to miss a couple of games this season due to injury."

"We're really taking it one day at a time, game by game." Senior Xavier's comments were short and reflective.

While Narit, Senior, is more direct: "Coming into the season, we were doubted, and we just want to prove a point."

The seniors answer their fellow students' questions with a veteran's poise, exemplifying our school motto: *Winning with Class*.

Tuesday: Practice

Tuesday, the practice is intense and more detailed but fluid. A lot of shooting games at game speed and defensive recovery drills.

An almost perfect session on the floor, followed with a great weight workout, foam rollers, and band stretching.

The ending to our weekly ritual of bonding together is the 5 minutes in ice. The training room, where the finishing touches take place, allows the guys to relax, too often tease one another, and cut up along with getting treatment on their lower extremities. I asked the trainers to make it as cold as possible, and Rachard's response: "We built for this, Coach."

Now, not a player is thinking that this could be our last ice bath treatment together as a team. But a "Kumbaya" moment fills the crowded space of guys awaiting their turn, and the sensation lingers within the room as the remaining two teammates step out of the freezing water when I click off the motor to the whirlpool for the final time this season.

Wednesday: Media & Chaos

Wednesday's anticipation of chaos and hurriedness doesn't disappoint. The scouting report is being assessed, the itinerary is updated by the minute, materials are checked out from our technology department, and the snack-gathering staff is buzzing. Things are popping in and around the basketball office.

Instructions are texted to the players concerning the ever-changing schedule of the day's occurrences: get out of class 6th period, change quickly for media, downstairs by 4:00 for team meeting. Enjoy this experience.

The media reminds us of picture day, a necessary evil we must deal with every year. It pushes those buttons, but at the end of the day, we will look back and cherish the memories made on this day.

Downstairs in the classroom, the finishing instructions and explanations are given to the players and coaches about tomorrow morning's activities and the travel plans, as our wrestling members and footballers walk through our meeting to their practice area. A normal daily occurrence, similar to the PESH cheer practice or the Golden Girls on the south court practicing their competition routines, separated only with a gigantic tarp net. Both mimicking our normal game-night experiences.

Coach Godwin pulls up Kahoot!—the teaching toolkit for engaging lessons and assignments—on San Antonio and The Alamo for the guys, as another bonding, fun thing. With it, he shares a video found on YouTube of a few teammates' performance during a talent show at their middle school five years ago. Great memories.

Before the fellas report to the locker room, I place a travel packing list in their lockers, but this list has a few minor tweaks. This list has **STATE** across the top. In the past, I used a regular "Tournament" or "Regionals" heading, but not this time.

Other add-ons: clothing for 3 days, 4th for travel; extra undergarments and t-shirts; sleeping attire; socks; both travel sweatsuits; toothpaste and brush; deodorant and cologne. Game bag, socks, shoes, and accessories too.

The excitement is otherworldly, but there is no storm on the horizon. Everything physical is in place—all the material, game-related or otherwise, is packed away. The only thing that remains is the coaches' personal belongings and mindset.

As I sit down at my desk, I glance at my phone. It's approaching 7:45 pm, and the realization comes to me that this season marks the 30th year Plano East made our only appearance in the state tournament. I knew it was in 1993, but the totality of it coinciding with 2023 hadn't really dawned on me until this very moment.

I guess with all the excitement and success of the season, a deep dive excluded the time frame. I take a deeper-than-usual gasp of air, and an even more humbling feeling flows throughout my being. "WOW." And I think to myself, *You're absolutely blessed to be on staff for this historical opportunity.*

Coach Wester, as an assistant on the Garland Naaman Forest 2011–2012 Final Four team, is the only coach who has participated in the state tournament in Austin, Texas. For Coach Godwin, Evans, Smith, and myself, this is our first, and I'm relieved.

Thursday Morning: Send-Off

Morning came in the blink of an eye. I packed the Tahoe, and before I know it, I'm commuting to Plano for our pep rally and send-off to San Antonio. About two miles into my drive, my playlist cues the next song—a childhood favorite, and this has to be a premonition. Bill Withers' *Lovely Day* commences, and in that instant, serenity. I press repeat five or six times until I reach campus, some 18 miles later. Thursday could not have been jump-started any other way.

All the players, managers, and trainers arrive at 8:15 for breakfast, and our bus conductor, Mr. Ron, pulls the charter up to the curb at 8:30. I hand over a copy of the itinerary, and Mr. Ron programs the times, destinations, and routes in waiting during the pep rally.

When loading the bus, a fan asks the players to sign a ball, a wooden panther, and a cap. A Next Level occurrence for sure.

Our resting place for the next three days will be the historic Emily Morgan Hotel, built on the Mexican battlegrounds in the early 1920s. It is located in downtown San Antonio, overlooking the Alamo, a few blocks from the infamous River Walk, and minutes away from the Alamodome—the site for the state tournament.

There is a backstory to the Emily Morgan Hotel. It is rumored to be the most haunted hotel in Texas. In 1836, the report states that over 600 men lost their lives close to the hotel, and the original building was for medical purposes and the care of psychological ailments. But we are here to play a couple of games.

UIL State Tournament Itinerary

March 7 – 10

Thursday, March 7

8:15 – Arrive at Plano East (Pack for 3 Days)

8:45 – Breakfast

9:00 – Pep Rally

9:15 – Walk Out/Send Off

9:30 – Depart PESH

1:00 – Practice at Leander Rouse High School

3:00 – Depart Leander Rouse/Lunch

5:50 – Arrive at Emily Morgan Hotel/Check-In

6:15 – Depart for the Alamodome to watch 5A Semi-Final

7:00 – SA Veteran's Memorial High vs. Killeen Ellison High

8:30 – Amarillo High vs. Lancaster High

10:00 – Depart Alamodome

10:30 – Dinner at Emily Morgan/Pizza

12:00 – Lights Out

Friday, March 8

8:30 – Wake Up/Breakfast in Emily Morgan

9:00 – Depart for Workout

9:30 – Shootaround at Paul Taylor Fieldhouse

10:15 – Arrive at Emily Morgan

10:45 – Depart Emily Morgan for Shootaround at Alamodome

11:30 – Shootaround – East goal

12:00 – Depart Alamodome/Lunch at Chipotle (Assistants pick up and bring back to hotel)

1:00 – Team Meeting Downstairs

2:30 – Off your feet/relax in your rooms

4:30 – Depart for Alamodome

5:00 – Arrive at Alamodome

7:00 – Tip Off vs. Mansfield Lake Ridge

8:30 – Watch Beaumont United vs. Stony Point

10:30 – Depart for Emily Morgan/Dinner from Gus's Famous Chicken (Assistants pick up)

12:00 – Lights Out

Saturday, March 9

8:30 – Wake Up/Breakfast

9:30 – Team Meeting Downstairs

10:00 – Depart Emily Morgan for Shootaround at Northside ISD Sports Complex

4:00 – Off your feet/relax in your rooms

5:15 – Depart for Alamodome

6:00 – Arrive at Alamodome

8:30 – Tip Off – vs. TBD

Sunday, March 10

9:00 – Wake Up

10:00 – Depart Emily Morgan for Plano

12:00 – Stop at Buc-ee's for Lunch/Snacks

3:30–4:00 – Arrive on Plano East campus

As instructed, the bus is to be fully packed and ready for departure after the pep rally no later than 9:15. The rally also includes The Panther Pride, our Special Olympic basketball team, coached by Anthony Ruttenburg, who qualified for their state tournament as well.

The rally starts with Coach Benedetto calling all of the student body to rise to their feet and turn on their phone lights while he introduces the players and coaches heading to the state tournaments with his energetic voice, like he's done the entire semester.

However, the walk to the bus—through the entire student body gathered alongside and around the bus—is exciting. *Having been a clapper and cheerer, this is a first for me as a participant, a coach, and it's quite moving in a manner of speaking.*

After everyone gets settled in, following the excitement of the sendoff, almost to the south Dallas side of downtown, I put *The*

Matrix DVD in to occupy or put the crew to sleep. I brought five DVDs total: three basketball flicks (*He Got Game*, *Hoosiers*, and *Coach Carter*) and *F9: The Fast Saga*. Thursday will be a long day, with three hours of travel time before practice at Leander Rouse High and three more hours until the bus reaches our destination, San Antonio.

Several players do the obvious—sleep. A few guys work on their NHS projects due after spring break, but most, including the coaches, watch the movie. About 12:15, 25 miles outside of Leander, those players sleeping are awakened, and the first stop along this journey falls into action.

Coach Krause, Leander Head Coach and former assistant to our Coach Evans at Vista Ridge High, allows East the use of their practice facilities for a mid-afternoon shootaround. After 20 minutes on the floor, Coach Wester wastes little time with the effort and lackadaisical attitude, stops a shooting station, and orders sprints. Multiple timed trips down and back—and the guys respectfully get back on track, finishing the practice in good spirits.

Lunch at Chick-fil-A, a team favorite meal, and then back on the road to San Antonio. Several hours later, approximately 5:15, the bus pulls up next to the Alamo, adjacent to the Emily Morgan Hotel, where the team will reside, hopefully, for the next couple of days.

Room assignments and check-in take some time, but the guys walk around the building and speak with other players, friends, even family members in town for the tournament. Beaumont United, Lipan, and Ponder are guests at the Emily Morgan Hotel as well. Coach Godwin, Coach Evans, and I get everything checked in. Coach Foley has the managers, and everyone is placed in a group text with the departure time for the Alamodome: 6:30 meet in the lobby.

Coach Smith, Jordan, and I get on the elevator on floor one, but it goes down to the basement level, then returns to floor one where Beaumont's Head Coach, David Green, his wife, and their big LSU football signee/center, Weston Davis, enter. We express gratitude. Then Coach Green turns to his wife and says, "Remember in June at the TABC, Coach said they would see us in March!" Mrs. Green smiles and agrees, "It's March." I speak up and comment to Coach Green, "This kid looks bigger than he did in June." And Coach responds, "If he can rebound like the one beside you, we will see you in the championship." It is a big compliment when another head coach publicly acknowledges your efforts. Jordan accepts the recognition with a grin and humility.

They exit the elevator on the 10th floor.

Coach Wester and I had discussed this evening on many occasions: having the team walk over to the Alamodome instead of taking the bus. Building yet more memories and adding another bonding opportunity with the fellas.

It is a much longer walk for us novices to San Antonio than for the frequent flyers, but the exercise serves its purpose. Nothing but laughs and teasing while working away the excess energy of the day. I'm not superstitious, but everyone now knows that Chima has no concern for splitting poles or walking under ladders. He enjoys pushing those buttons.

After getting directions to the player/coach entrance gate and receiving the best security pat down upon entrance, our group walks the elongated Alamodome facility—an absolute monstrosity of a building, some two hundred yards from the locker room area to the court entrance.

The aroma in the air from the Alamodome is intoxicating. The atmosphere is energizing and refreshingly captivating. It is exactly how I imagined it would be, seventeen years later—but this time as a participant, not as a spectator—completing a self-fulfilling prophecy.

Arriving in the first quarter of the 5A Semi-Finals game, Veteran's Memorial vs. Killeen Ellison, as the team approaches the floor area, a familiar cry rings out from the stands: "PLANO, PLANO, EAST, EAST. PLANO, PLANO, EAST, EAST." The echoes gain participants, and the chant is even louder with the third rendition. Further acknowledgment that the Panthers have entered the building, as the audience's heads turn in our direction.

I lean over towards Xavier, in Narit's direction, and whisper: "I told you so. We made you guys a promise last spring, that when you enter the Dome, *All Eyez on Me*, per Tupac, this would happen." Both could only grin and smile as they follow their teammates into the players' section of the arena. I played it off, acting as if it wasn't a surprise, but that verbal acknowledgment is huge and firmly solidifies that we have arrived. The guys soak in the attention.

Along the route into the seating area, I happen to see coaches and friends in the basketball world I've crossed paths with over the years: Coach Mayo and Coach Mauldin, Skyline and Garland Lakeview, standing courtside where we entered. Coach Mays, South Oak Cliff, and Coach Johnson, Kimball, to their left, and a few familiar referees among the bunch. *This is next level,* I thought. These iconic state champion coaches will watch Plano East play on the biggest stage Friday night. And I'm not humble in the moment— I'm feeling the juice.

With one minute remaining in the third quarter and Lancaster beating up on Memorial, Coach Wester texts the group to head to the bottom of the gym and exit the same area we entered. As we rise, another supporter bellows out: "PLANO, PLANO, EAST, EAST," and we exit the arena.

About a hundred yards into the walk back to the Emily Morgan Hotel, the suggestion to call Mr. Ron, our bus driver, is made. Ten minutes later, the group is scooped up and escapes the lengthy trudge around Interstate 35.

Team dinner—pizza and such—is on the bottom floor of the hotel, in a conference room assigned to Plano East. We will conduct all team functions there. The video screen and other miscellaneous items already occupy space along the back wall. It has been a long day.

10:00 – In your rooms
12:00 – Lights Out

Coach Smith is burning the midnight oil, tidying up the scouting report on Lake Ridge, while I doze off watching NCAA conference tournament recaps on ESPN. But during our sleep, it gets unbearably cold, leaving me to put on socks and sweats.

In the morning, about 7:30, on my way to breakfast, I report the room temperature issue to the front desk and see Coach Godwin eating by himself. We're both early risers, morning people, and with the day's task at hand—a semifinals game and all—who could lie around and do nothing? Not me. Anxiety is winning, but a beautiful sunshine is welcoming. Coach Godwin and I take a walk over to the Alamo for a quick look before the wake-up/team breakfast at 8:30.

The five-minute walk across the corridor, paired with a beautiful morning, gives one pause while reading the brass monuments describing the battle of the Alamo. Even more breathtaking is the smallness of the building for such a historical battle.

While reading the stone, I take several pictures and text them to my wife, Rebecca, an 8th-grade history teacher, who's home packing to travel to her favorite city and meet up with her parents, Don and Sandy, for our game tonight. Also, my sister Allison and her two sons, Devin and Ty, will be in attendance for the second game, Stony Point vs. Beaumont United, at 8:30. Allison and Ty— both working at Stony Point, where Ty graduated—are eager to watch.

Other expected family members include my daughter, Quinae, her husband Jamie, and their three children, Kaiden, Karter, and Kinsley; my son Chauncey; cousin Jason; and nephews, Coach Derrick Richardson and his brother Jon. A total family affair.

No one needs to be called or texted. The entire entourage is punctual and ready to board the bus for the first of two shootarounds—9:30 at Paul Taylor Fieldhouse and the second at the

Alamodome, 35 minutes away, scheduled for 11:30. Lunch back at the hotel: Chipotle at noon or shortly thereafter.

All four 6A teams are at shootaround: Beaumont United and Stony Point waiting in the stands, us and Lake Ridge on the court. Our coaches couldn't help noticing the other coaching staffs and their assistants, at midcourt, transfixed on our players warming up.

During the team meeting, on video and in the scouting report, it is discovered they only want to play eight players—advantage us. They play with a lot of emotion, sometimes too much, which could work in our favor—advantage us. They are very aggressive and make few adjustments within the game. If it comes down to mental toughness, we should also have the advantage there.

The players are dismissed and given a time to report to the lobby for departure to the Alamodome at 4:30, while the coaches turn their focus on situational plays, defensive philosophy, rotations, and key individual matchups. Then we retire to our rooms for a quick nap and shower.

Two hours later, the team is awakened and refreshed. The managers and trainers are waiting downstairs in the lobby, and the coaches have prepared the squad to handle anything Lake Ridge has to offer tonight. I hand out the scouting report as we wait for the bus.

After a brief look outside the hotel, Mr. Ron pulls the bus just past the front lobby entrance door, and the team loads up for the Alamodome. "I'll get us there in 30 minutes or less, depending on the traffic," he says.

The bus arrives at the Alamodome ahead of schedule, but Mr. Ron isn't allowed to park because the loading dock is full. We circle the parking lot a few times until other vehicles are moved, giving Mr. Ron a spot to back into. Following our traditional routine of exiting the bus, the coaches first, we fist pump one another, then do the same with each manager, the trainers, and each player. I collect the scouting reports from the players as well—another uniting and focus pillar.

4A Stafford vs. Dallas Oak Cliff Faith Family is playing their semifinal game.

Another extensive bag check, pat down—"This is ridiculous," I think—but today's entrance into the Dome is **first class.** We are given the "red carpet" treatment. Our team is appointed our own UIL host and hostess to personally escort us everywhere we need access. Whatever happened the evening before is forgotten this time through.

"Dang it, this is big time," I whisper to Coach Evans as we're led to our locker room.

Game 39: Plano East vs. Mansfield Lake Ridge @ Alamodome – San Antonio, Texas

The hostess advises Coach Smith, who tells me, and I pass it along to Coach Wester: our first call of duty is to quickly change into our uniforms and coaching attire for the official team photo before our game preparations begin.

Upon returning to our locker room, I get the old-school music flowing at low volume as the fellas stretch together at the end of the room. There is tension among the guys, but that's to be expected when playing in your first state semifinal game—the second in school history. I have Seth and Ammani pass out the scout as the locker room clock reads 40 minutes and counting.

The one thing on the minds of coaches is to not allow a repeat of last weekend's Regional Semifinal with Eaton to emerge today with Lake Ridge. A premium effort is concentrated on getting off to a great first-quarter start, beginning with knowing their personnel and strengths.

Starters:

- #0 White – Probably the weakest of the group.
- #4 McMillan – Energetic player, always looking to score, nice pull-up jumper.
- #5 Rose – Emotional player.

248

- #10 Eze – Big, aggressive, physical; will charge over you.
- #22 Alexander – Aggressive on defense, handsy and physical.

Defensively: They play physical and out of control. Some might label them dirty, with a chip on their shoulder. They are lengthy and aggressive, get into passing lanes, and tip a lot of balls. **Keys:** Move the ball, cut, and set screens. The more the ball reverses sides, the easier buckets we will get. *(Shoot the ball with confidence.)*

Offensively: They run a motion style of play. Miss a lot of easy shots when challenged or with contact. They don't shoot it well but crash the boards hard.
Keys: Block out. Rebound like state champions. Communicate with each other. *(10 points or less each quarter, 40 points total.)*

Don't get emotional. Play the game and everything else will take care of itself.

Then we play the visionary game. The guys close their eyes and I ask: *Who is getting into the passing lane? Who is stealing that pass? Who is helping in the paint? Taking the charge? Diving on the floor for a loose ball? Who is talking on the bench?*

Coach Wester reenters the room and takes over the meeting, giving his overall vision and the most appropriate analysis to date:

We only need to be one point up at the end of this game. Go out and play like state champions play.

1 – 2 – 3 Eastside, 4 – 5 – 6 State Champs.

Twenty-one minutes and counting on the game clock as we exit the dressing room.

Our particular locker room for today's game is the farthest of the four available dressing rooms, so the hostess arrives a few minutes early to escort the players to the entrance area of the court. When the team walks onto the floor, a humongous roar from an already large crowd echoes the excitement of a state semifinal game.

The atmosphere is better than anything we could've expected. The Eastside contingency shows up, as well as basketball lovers from all over Texas, wanting to witness the #1 state-ranked, #2 nationally ranked Panthers for themselves.

Questions run wild: *Are they really that good? Can they close the deal? They don't have any star power players!* Prognosticators, sports columnists, podcasters, and bettors weigh in or wager on the possibility—or the improbable—perfect season. Others hate on the reality that this may be one of the best high school basketball teams ever to play in Texas. **40–0 gets them into the conversation.**

As we enter the court, I see Mr. and Mrs. McAfee, our former principal and attendee at every playoff game, standing courtside and cheering as the fellas begin our warmup routine. Our eyes meet. I walk to his area; he does the same toward me. We embrace and shake hands like we did the day he hired me, 26 years ago at Plano East. Pleasantries are exchanged. Under the basketball goal, I retreat, ready to switch to the next drill, *Fist Shooting,* as I raise both hands above my head, signaling the action desired.

Sixteen minutes and counting.

Half court, I call out. Each player jogs to midcourt two times, stretching out their legs. Motion Shooting—and the guys roll into the action like they have performed 39 other times this season without fail. "Shot fake, roll back, get to the nail." Half court, two jogs to midcourt. Then the three-point/free-throw shooting for eight minutes—four with the guards and four with the bigs—as I start my step-counting walk around the edge of the court, sizing up the opponent. Upon each circling, I shout out "Rotate," and the players change shooting spots on command.

Eight minutes and counting.

A couple of coaches or fans, it happens every so often, ask me what I was screaming at the players, and my response is that I am directing them to put up as many shots as possible—game shots, at game speed, in a short time frame, on command. "It's rhythmic," I tell them.

On every trip around the court, I notice the Lake Ridge players and a few of their assistants watching our warmup routine instead of preparing themselves for the game. Quite often their players are walking back to the lines and watching our warmup, reacting to my voice and not focusing on their own immediacy.

Along midcourt and adjacent to the scorer's table, I greet Coach Perry, a Lake Ridge assistant to Coach Mitchell, and in 2004 the Head Coach at Irving High when his team defeated us in the Regional Quarterfinals. In our impromptu visit, Coach Perry provides the coach-speak: "We're hoping to keep it close," or something to that effect. My response, while shaking my head: "Not today, Coach. Not today." Then I continue my fact-gathering walk around.

Three minutes and counting.

I share with our coaches on the last walk around. I find my wife and in-laws in the huge black-and-gold rendering of the East contingent that braved the roads to South Central Texas. I see our principals, board members, and students—several that grace the gym daily—and I usher them out, per Coach Wester. Their support is unwavering.

After the player introductions and before the tip, a slight breeze hits me, and I get a rush of nervous feelings like never before, as a player or as a coach. I can't take another walk to shed the anxiety or mask the emotions; I can only wipe my head as the sweat bubbles atop my baldness begin to form.

As I settle into the extra-small chair lining the bench area—the first chair next to the scorer's table, Coach Wester to my immediate left, Coach Godwin, Coach Evans, and so forth—a slight breeze hits me, and as if 15 years were lifted off my shoulders, I inhale and exhale the deepest of deep breaths. *Finally, we are here.* The reality marinates in my brain.

With one of the two personal goals accomplished, and 32 minutes of competition to determine our fate, it is worth the price of admission.

From the onset of the toss, there's a third-party flow within the game. During the first three possessions: turnover, missed shot, turnover. Four stoppages in under two minutes due to bodies clashing. Physicality is an understatement—we should be wearing helmets and shoulder pads. For the first time in months, our players need to adjust to the refereeing style and their calls. But the fellas in the heat of the battle show little concern or lose their composure. Meanwhile, our bench is losing it.

An evenly fought first period ends 9–9 as both teams struggle to put the ball in the net. Lake Ridge shoots 4/8, 1–4 from deep, with 2 turnovers and 3 fouls. East is 4/15, 1–3 from deep, 4 turnovers, but with 9 second-chance opportunities.

East adjusts midway through the second period, and the defense seizes control of the good-shooting Eagles (48%). The Panthers, who can only manage to shoot 37% (3/10 from distance), lead at intermission, 26–22.

There is no panic in the locker room—from Coach Wester or any other coaches. They shot the ball well, and we didn't. "No worries. They won't shoot like that this half, and we need to see the ball go in." His clearer message is to keep shooting the ball when a makeable shot presents itself. Rebound the ball like champions, get every 50/50 ball, and make game-winning plays on defense.

And like Nostradamus, Coach Wester's prediction comes to fruition. The Panthers' defense plays to their abnormal abilities, placing a cap on the Eagles' offensive efforts. East holds Lake Ridge to 4/11 shooting in the third period (10 points total) while going 8/17, 3–7 behind the arc, and scoring 20. A commanding 46–32 advantage into the final stanza.

East controls the tempo and clock in the fourth period. DJ, Jordan, and Narit score the final points in the game, taking the quarter 16–15. Isaiah emerges with 6 boards, 4 assists, 5 steals, and 0 points. Unfortunately, the quarter is marred with foul stoppages. DJ fouls out of a contest for the first time this season, and as a team, the Panthers collect 16 fouls while Lake Ridge totals 21.

In the final minutes, the fouls become personal, almost flagrant, when Jon and Narit are whistled for technicals following a hard foul. As the pushing and grabbing rev up, our coaches quickly lean in on our bench players, preventing them from crossing the sidelines. Per UIL rules, if a player leaves the bench area, he/she is automatically disqualified for the next contest. Equally important, if a player is ejected or given a second technical during a contest, he/she is disqualified also.

With all the commotion going on right in front of our bench, Coach Wester is trying to get answers. One ref walks to the scorer's table to render his call while the other two refs walk to each sideline, seeking the head coach.

UIL Assistant AD Joseph Garman, sitting at the scorer's table, reacts to the mini skirmish, sees my reaction, and pulls me to the side. First, stating, "Good job, Coach," then whispering in my ear: "Coach, two technicals were awarded to your team. #2 and #11. If they receive a second, they will not be eligible for the championship tomorrow."

I quickly grab Xavier and Rachard for Narit and Jon. Coach Wester, still trying to get an explanation, doesn't see the technical determination. He turns to me and asks, "Why are you subbing?" I respond, "Narit and Jon were assessed a tech." Coach is beside himself again. The first occurs when a charge call goes against Jordan earlier in the fourth quarter on a fast break—a bad call, nonetheless.

The refs regain control, and the game is resumed.

As the buzzer sounds, marking the end of a hard-fought North Texas semifinal contest, the team members briefly but hysterically jump into each other's arms, slapping hands and such, then calmly line up to shake the Lake Ridge coaches' and players' hands before sprinting toward the huge crowd of fans in the black-and-gold section on the home side of the Alamodome.

A loud *PLANO PLANO, EAST EAST* is shouted from the stands—but this time it rings familiar and from a voice dear to the Eastside family. It's Mr. Mike Malone, our former East booster president and father of two graduate ballers, Mickey and last season's point guard, Nate. A battle cry that will forever reverberate in the ears of the Plano East community.

In the meantime, the hostess and ushers are attempting to hurry along the celebration, in preparation for the second 6A semifinal contest between Stony Point and Beaumont United, set for 8:30 and now behind schedule. They guide our players, coaches, and cheerleaders—holding a sign that reads *(39–0 Semi-Finals Champs)*—to center court for a group photo. Congratulatory texts and calls begin to fill my phone.

I also walk over to the Plano East section afterwards to hug and kiss my wife, Rebecca, my in-laws, my son Chauncey, my daughter Quinae, and her children, Kaiden, Karter, and Kinsley. I exchange handshakes and high fives with our administrators, students, and fans—whoever I make eye contact with—but my immediate plan is to bring my grandsons onto the court to be a part of the celebration. The belief is for them to be in this moment as well, to feel and see what hard work and dedication can lead to. More often than not, sights and sounds beget dreams. I'm planting seeds.

I retrieve Kaiden and Karter from the seating area and begin to exit the gymnasium floor when my nephew Ty, leaning over the railing, attracts my attention. He leads us to the heart of the Stony Point section, where his mother, my sister Allison, is seated for their game. We embrace for a few seconds. She says, "Congratulations." I comment, "Good luck." Both oddly true, but we could feel the animosity from the Stony Point fandom. The group only sees the Plano East Basketball monogram on my sweater. Most are unaware that we are siblings and could care less. They are here to cheer for their Tigers.

The boys and I say our goodbyes and trot to the locker room at the other end of the Alamodome. Sharing these moments with the grandchildren is so special.

Mansfield Lake Ridge 45 - Plano East 61

LRHS: McMillan 20 pts, White 8 pts, Rose 8 pts, Alexander 6 pts, Eze 5 pts

PEHS: DJ 15 pts, 10 rbds; Jordan 13 pts, 5 rbds; Narit 11 pts; Xavier 9 pts, 6 rbds

Plano East 39–0, State Semi-Finals Champions

Three major takeaways in the second half:

1. East's defense is the unsung hero.
2. The referee crew, who only managed to call five fouls on both teams in the first half, blows the whistle 32 times in the second.
3. The three-point disparity: the Panthers shoot 7–19 while the Eagles go 1–12.

Inside the locker room, the players quietly undress, waiting for Coach Wester to return from the UIL postgame press conference that he, Narit, Jordan, and DJ attended. The water bottles hidden under chairs, beside towels and travel bags, provided by Coach Foley, are unleashed as the coaches enter and the celebration restarts.

Lights flashing, dancing on the tables, jerseys waving over their heads—acting like little children in a candy store.

After the staged celebration, Coach addresses the team, and everyone gathers their belongings and heads to the stands to meet with family and friends, and to watch our next opponent for the state championship tomorrow night. There is little concern about the next game or the opponent—too much excitement is taking place, and we are soaking it up.

Fifteen minutes later, and just prior to the tip of the second 6A semifinals game, what appears to be everyone from East Plano is standing in the lobby area. The other staff coaches and their family members—momentarily—we find ourselves surrounded by hordes of supporters and East students who made the bus trip from campus for tonight's game. The atmosphere is surreal. A large group of Panthers has gathered outside in the foyer by the restrooms, waiting for the remaining students, staff, and chaperones to load the buses for the ride home at 9:00 pm. Principal Eppler mentions that a Saturday bus for the Alamodome will be en route, with a departure time of 1:00 pm for the 8:30 state championship.

During intermission, dinner from Gus's Famous Chicken is ordered and, after the third period, our entourage departs the Alamodome for the Emily Morgan. The meal arrives shortly afterward. Everyone eats well and enjoys the camaraderie.

10:00 – In your room

12:00 – Lights Out

My wife joins us, and we hang out downstairs and around the hotel for several hours before tiring. She took the day off from teaching 8th grade and drove in from Celina, battling car troubles along the way. I walk her, not far away, to the La Quinta Inn, where she and the in-laws are staying. San Antonio is Rebecca's favorite city to visit. She once resided and taught in the area for three years, almost 20-plus years ago.

An 11:00 coaches' meeting is texted for the basement—to touch base, make sure of the plans for tomorrow, and celebrate again on today's accomplishment. We did it. Reached the goal of earning the right to play in the last game of the season, on the last night, for a state championship title.

A checklist of things must be covered:

- Make sure Mr. Ron is updated.
- Get the home jerseys washed. (Hotel says they will wash them.)
- Contact the Paul Taylor Facility or Northside ISD for shootaround.

The season's goal, from jump, was to play in the final game of the year in San Antonio.

"39 down and one more to go!" I emphatically shout.

About 3:30, I'm awakened by a noise, and it is freezing cold again in the room. I don't bother calling; I walk down to the lobby for a second time in two days to report the problem. A maintenance man accompanies me to the room, checks the wall gauge, and inspects the AC cooling system in the restroom ceiling. I fall back asleep shortly later.

Saturday morning, I'm up early—7:00—because something crazy is going on in my room. I head over to the La Quinta for breakfast with my wife before the guys' mandatory 8:30 wakeup call. I stop by the basement to check out the scene and see Coach Evans and Coach Godwin already eating, laptops open and reviewing the scout. I share that the jerseys are complete, Mr. Ron is aware of the plans for our shootaround, and complain about my room, the rumors of it being haunted, and tell them I will return within the hour.

8:30 – Wakeup/Breakfast – Everyone is on time. A very, very good sign.

9:30 – Team Meeting

All video clips. Coach notices that the Tigers have borrowed one of our inbound plays and added it to their playbook. Nothing new from them. We know who their #1 player is, Josiah. We know their shooters, Buntyn and Short, and how they get to their spots. We know who handles their sets, Alan and Goodlet. And we know their coach.

Not much is said. No music. No scouting report. Only repetitional visuals. The mental aspect of the game is delicate and must be championed. The little things count.

11:00 – Free Time
12:30 – Depart for Northside ISD Sports Complex
1:00 – Arrive at Northside ISD Sports Complex

A great morning practice begins with ball-handling drills (10 minutes). Form shooting (10 minutes). Race to 50 from the corner (10 minutes). Race to 50 from the wing. 5-on-0 (10 minutes). Two groups, foam rollers and band stretching (7 minutes each).

2:30 – Depart for Emily Morgan
4:00 – Off your Feet/Relax in your Room
4:30 – Team Dinner/Chipotle
5:15 – Depart for Alamodome/Tour Around Town

Coach Wester asks Mr. Ron for the scenic tour around the city of San Antonio, to mimic a district road trip. Coach wanted us out of the hotel and to burn as much time as possible before we walk into the Alamodome. Mr. Ron does exactly that. A 45-minute drive to nowhere. But I utilize the time by picking a playlist mixture of old songs and new artists—describing living in the moment, having this one opportunity to prove oneself, positive vibes, shining when the lights are brightest. And music to get the blood flowing.

Old songs: *In the Air Tonight, Under Pressure, Regulate* **Artists who speak on fighting through hard times and emerging victorious:** Eminem (*Till I Collapse*), Drake (*God's Plan* and *Headlines*), Nicki Minaj (*Moment 4 Life*), Kanye West (*All of the Lights*), and our introduction cut—Mystikal (*Here I Go*). Not only for the beat, but songs with a message that motivates.

6:00 – Arrive at Alamodome
4A State Championship game is in progress.

The bus pulls into Parking Area 1, closest to the loading dock, the back entrance to the check-in station. Everyone stands up at the same time, almost in unison, anxious to de-bus for the biggest sporting opportunity in school history. But all is calm on the South Texas front. Individually, each person has their bags checked and is wanded. Our hostess is waiting inside the entrance door and escorts our group to the designated locker room for the final game of the 2023–2024 season.

Our walk to the lockers isn't as far as yesterday, which is surprisingly unexpected considering the last two days of cross-country events we participated in. What is noticed is the size of the locker room—a feature that was overlooked in the midst of the semifinal preparations. This room is ginormous; it's the biggest of big time. Each player has a larger-than-usual changing station, and the floor is carpeted, like ours. Coach Smith and I drop off the travel bag with the ropes, foam rollers, and towels for the players to begin their stretching before we head to the coaches' dressing area to change.

2 hours and counting.

The hostess communicates that the schedule is behind about 30 minutes.

After settling in, the players begin their pregame rituals of machine massaging—each has his own massager, and it can sound like an auto body shop if you walk in at the right time. Some jump rope, stretch, and apply Icy Hot. That stuff can wake the dead. They see Coach Foley for treatment and taping, and a couple others sit back and relax. In the meantime, the coaches retire to the adjacent room to prepare the books, boards, or dress for the game.

1 hour, 30 minutes and counting.

Some of the fellas take a walk outside our locker area to the television down the corridor and observe the 5A title game being played.

40 minutes and counting.

All the team members are called back to the locker room. I hand the scouting report to Coach Simpson, and he distributes it to every player and coach in the room. Coach Foley is handed a report—he doesn't need it and has never before received one—but he takes the counter-strategy and places the paper on the table. For some odd reason, I'm noticing there are extras to go around, but that's my focus; the smallest of details were surfacing.

Tonight, there is no tension in the locker room. No wandering of the minds, no shenanigans. Only reminders about Stony Point, all the memories of two dates: December 30th and, not to mention, the TABC in June, have combined to create a scenario that no matter what, this team knows they can win this game.

Just one loss, officially on paper, separates the ball clubs. However, the 25-point blowout at TABC reigns rent-free in the minds of those who made that DFW trip. It isn't just the defeat, but how we defeated them—a swarming defense with easy buckets on the other end. The same game is ready to be deployed this evening.

When we sit down to read through the report, not any of the players or coaches are thinking this is the final time. Business as usual on game day. "The most intense and the best-focused person in the entire dome tonight is going to be me. Playing every possession as if my life depends on it."

The first song on the playlist is *God's Plan.*

We match up favorably with the Tigers—player for player, scheme for scheme—but we already know who's the better ball club. Who is the tougher team, the tougher player—mentally and physically. And at the end of the game tonight, WE will SHOW who's the toughest team. The tougher team will win.

Spoken into existence.

As our customary reading of the scout report, I routinely pick a senior to read the opponent's offensive scheme, their strengths, and how they score the ball. I pick another senior to read through their defensive philosophy and a third for the reserves. But tonight, I will read the entire report.

There is nothing new to this plan. We know what they do and who their focal players are. I initiate with our assignments and player matchups as follows; then I include the boldest of statements: "We have already won this game. We only have to put in the two hours of work to claim our SHIP."

Round Rock Stony Point – Starters

- **#4 Guyton, 5'6 Senior, PG, Primary ball handler.** Isaiah, pressure him from the tip. If he goes to the sideline to talk with Coach Thompson, go with him. Make him uncomfortable. Rachard, he cannot guard you—no one on this team can. Attack them every chance you get.

- **#1 Buntyn, 6'0 Junior, Guard, Shooter.** Jon, no open shots, then make him guard you. He doesn't want to play defense that long. He will lose you on ball reversals. Shoot your shots.

- **#3 Goodlet, 6'4 Senior, Wing, Best Defender.** Jordan, keep him off the glass on defense and do you. Show everyone who is the best rebounding guard in the state.

- **#10 Short, 6'2 Junior, Guard, Best Shooter.** Xavier, your first priority is to lock his butt up. Make him earn every point he gets. No open shots. Put his ass on lockdown. Xavier nods his head in agreement. Then make him guard you. Shoot the open shot and crash the offensive glass. Narit, when you enter the game, this is your job as well. Score the ball. He doesn't have the same effort on defense.

- **#2 Moseley, 6'8 Senior, Best Player, #1 Ranked Player in the State.** DJ, you whipped his ass in June. You kicked his ass at the CBI. What do we expect you to do to him tonight? DJ responds, "Kick his ass." No smiles, nor blinks an eye, because this is the expectation of each player.

Reserves

- **#11 Cruz, 6'3 Junior.** Aggressive driver, can score the ball.
- **#24 Hueitt, 6'9 Junior.** Post, who can shoot the 3. Take him off the dribble from the perimeter. He will play physical—use that against him.
- **#23 John, 6'3 Sophomore.** Aggressive on offense, suspect on defense. Attack him.

Offensively: They will not play past three reversals. Shoot the ball. If you cannot score the ball, give it to someone who can. Then cut hard and screen harder for your teammate. Move and share the ball. Don't pass up open shots. Do I care who scores the points? No. But I do care if you play selfishly. Do not be that player tonight.

Now—"Everyone, close your eyes," I ask. "Who is going to take that charge? Who is getting up the line for a deflection or steal? Who is diving on the floor for that loose ball?" Questions for each to visualize before completing the task—and things they've been doing all season.

At 8:18 pm, I see Coach Wester enter the main locker room area, and I relinquish to our leader. The players, sitting in the attentive position—except DJ, who is on the floor getting in his final stretching—listen as Coach states: "This is what we've been working for since November 1st." He reminds the team, "Every one

268

of you knows what he has to do for us to be successful." He calls for our team circle and says… and everyone gets up to follow…

1–2–3 Eastside. 4–5–6 State Champs.

Then we wait as the 5A championship celebration concludes.

What seems like an hour—but is actually 10 minutes—and our hostess knocks on the door and hand motions to the players, a come-on gesture, says "Let's go." It's time to make our way towards the gymnasium floor.

There's a burst of excitement when the directive, the sound of "Plano East, it's your turn," the hostess confirms, and many of the guys exit the room in pursuit. Almost all were in the hallway when Narit glances to our right—not that far but at least two locker rooms down—and sees the Stony Point entourage gathering outside their holding area too.

Narit, a bit animated or highly spirited, remembers the Coach Holtz story I shared with them last season in the Allen tournament. "Coach Thomas, Coach Thomas, why are we going in first?" Narit asked. "Aren't we the MAIN attraction!" he expresses. And in an instant, the team slows the walking pace to a halt in response. "Tell the hostess that we aren't going in first," and Narit complies. "Ma'am, we're not going first!" The hostess stops, and our team moves to the empty area at the corner ending of the intersecting hallway, midway to the court. Storytelling revisited and rooted firmly.

Meanwhile in tow, Stony Point is following their hostess's lead towards the gym when several of our guys begin to hum and sing to the tune of *Headlines* by Drake: *they know, they know, they know...* as they walk past. This causes a few word exchanges from both players and coaches, but the mood is quite definitely set for a heated battle. There is NO love lost here. Just one defeat separates our giants.

If yesterday was a hill, and we got over it, today is the mountain and we will need that same energy and more. The attendance for this game should be the biggest thus far and, with live streaming, who knows how many fans will finally see the Panthers put on a show. It's for the title. For all the bragging rights that come with it. **40–0, possibly being added into the conversations as one of the best seasons in Texas high school basketball history.**

22 minutes and counting.

As we approach the small entranceway under the stadium bleachers, before the arena, a few players notice the flashes from the cone-hidden cameras taking live photos. Didn't remember them being there the day before and could care less now. However, a couple of players pose and sprint to catch up to the group as we enter on our fan side of the arena, and the roar of the crowd grows to a feverish pitch as the Panther players take the floor for warmup.

Adjacent to our bench, there is a large contingent of people wearing the black and gold. Apparently, the enthusiasm from last night's semifinal victory over Lake Ridge attracts an even bigger student turnout for the 6-hour return trip to San Antonio for the championship game.

With Round Rock being in close proximity to the "Alamo City," this scene should provide a Tiger home court feel, an advantage of sorts to help intimidate and give a level charge, but it doesn't. This is a Plano East partisan crowd. "What a great turnout we have from the Eastside of Plano," Coach Godwin acknowledges.

Per DFW *Inside High School Sports* feature in January, our nationally ranked Panthers have been seeking to complete the Plano ISD trifecta—taking down any competition that stands in front of us for several months. Not true. We have been on this quest since February 24, 2023, and now we are 20 minutes away from this reality.

From the moment we touch the playing surface, the sharing of eye contact and facial respect reciprocates the magnitude of the game. Those sitting on the floor—from UIL officials, former legendary coaches, to other celebrities, like Tracy McGrady, a former NBA great. From a short distance away, I hear my name, Greg Thomas, being summoned.

The familiar voice instantly grabs my attention; the rapport seeking to be recognized is from my childhood neighbor. Memories of the 10-year-old baseball teammate, high school quarterback room teammate, and now the leader of many, Superintendent Dr. Steve Flores.

We shake hands and greet each other like the long-lost friends we are. Although brief, a few memories come and go quickly—a game needs to be played. The early exercise of our warmup routine is finishing as I move under the basketball, signaling to jog to half court, two times, as they have perfected the last three years, with me directing them or not.

Walking to my left, I see Dr. Watson, the Head Principal of Stony Point. We embrace and exchange pleasantries for a couple of minutes. I first met Dr. Watson 10 years ago while attending my nephew Tyree's football game, and we have remained in touch ever since.

12 minutes and counting.

I begin my walk around the court, and the players move on with the warmup—'bigs on the outside and smalls inside.' The routine change because DJ asked. He wants to get up more perimeter shots in pregame, something we discussed in the locker room.

The normal trek around reveals little except the glare of Stony Point is one of anticipation, not fear. Most teams, during our pregame, show signs of weariness or doubt. But tonight, the Tigers, who displayed the deer-in-headlights look in previous meetings, give no indication. Their outward appearance seems formidable.

On my third trip around, I see my family members in the stands. I recognize other coaches and acquaintances as well, but I had not seen the person and voice of Texas high school state championship games, Craig Way. A bucket list missed.

2 minutes and counting.

The team gathers at the free throw lane, arm in arm, like we have done 39 times this season and for 7 seniors, 110 times the previous 3 years…

HARD WORK, PAYS OFF,
Hard Work, Pays Off,
Hard work. Paying Off.

I walk away from the group saying, "Don't be denied. Be in the moment."

They finish the unity circle with, "Who got my back? I got your back," led by Narit, but it epitomizes the brotherhood.

Game 40: Round Rock Stony Point vs Plano East @ Alamodome, San Antonio, Texas

State Championship

The scene is everything it's supposed to be, and then some. You think about it, but in the moment that conception vanishes. The past sixteen years, I have turned the television to Fox Sports Southwest at 2:30 and watched the 4A/5A/6A championships play out from the comforts of my living room, often visualizing East in this very ball game. Having deep images, thoughts, and conversations with myself on every possession. Questioning every strategic coaching move. Asking myself, what coaching adjustments would I make? Should we change the defense, or not? Who do I substitute?

But today, those simple questions can be asked and answered in real time. I'm not 5 hours away on my couch, eating homemade sandwiches and drinking tea. Finally, I'm on staff with a team who is playing on the last day of the season, in the biggest game of their lives, and for a title. Dreams do come true.

The announcing of the players sounds different—and it isn't. The National Anthem seems clearer—it isn't. Giving dap with the fellas is harder—and that's intentional. But the environment and atmosphere are electric.

9:05 - Tip Off

Josiah and DJ jump at center court, and Stony Point has the first crack at the lead—a rebound to Xavier. Isaiah signals an overload set, and after a few passes, Jon delivers a perfect assist to a jumping DJ for a layup. East with the 2–0 lead.

The Tigers tie the game on the following possession and take a 2-point lead with a pressure double-team at the top of the circle, causing a turnover for an uncontested Josiah layup. Stony Point 4–2.

It is the Josiah-DJ battle off the bat. Josiah scores 8 of the 11 Tiger points and teammate Hueitt adds 3, rounding out their total, while DJ bolsters 7 of the first 9 for East. DJ scores on a couple of assists from Jordan—a paint bunny followed with a three-pointer from the wing. Rachard enters midway through the first period and makes an immediate impact, scoring 4 points off dribble drives, and Jordan's putback gives the Panthers a 15–11 lead after one.

The second quarter is a battle of wills. *Can we will them down?* Who will be the tougher ball club? Stony Point wins the transition scoring, 8–6 in the quarter, but shoots 2/9 from distance. East wins the rebound, second-chance points, free throws, paint scoring, 18–

12, and points off turnovers, 14–5, for the 29–24 intermission advantage.

The coaches retreat to the coach's office, and the players take seats in their chosen lockers, everyone breathing heavily after jogging a football field for the break. After a short meeting, the consensus on defense is to continue helping on the backside, pressure the passers, keep active hands, and get every 50/50 ball.

They have no answer for DJ or our ability to rebound. Crash the offensive glass and score the easy shots, our 4s and 5s (layups). This is the dagger to their hearts. "The tougher team will win this game," Coach Wester's last words.

1–2–3 Eastside. 4–5–6 State Champs.

Cross-country jog to the court we go!

3 minutes and counting. 3rd Quarter.

I walk over to Coach Wester and hand him the electronic board. No one is in foul trouble for us, but #3 Goodlet has three for them. Both teams have four timeouts. I also give him and Coach Godwin the official stat sheet, provided by the UIL statisticians. Notice: they are 2/9 from three and only shot four free throws in the half. They have makes of layups and jump shots—not very physical.

The third quarter begins like the second ended. The Panthers' defense, like they have done all season in the period after break, raises their level of intensity and applies more pressure on the opposing players. *That's why we do all those sprints and mile runs.* When our opponents are winding down, we are in second gear. They tire, and we bring in five more guys—faster and more active. DJ and Rachard each knock down a timely three-pointer to thwart the Tigers' comeback hopes.

Other than the #4 Guyton and Hueitt threes, Stony Point finds it difficult to score. They manage a 9–0 run with those makes, but the closest the Tigers get to the Panthers is six points in that stretch. The only lead the Tigers have in the contest came at the 6:00 mark of the first period. East wins the quarter, 12–11, and leads 41–35. However, the lead has a double-digit feel.

There is no fourth-quarter drama. The Panthers hold the Tigers to three shot attempts and four turnovers, and score on consecutive possessions, building a 10-point upper hand with five minutes to go. DJ scores the Panthers' last made field goal with the big clock reading 6:18 in the final stanza.

After another missed three opportunities by the Tigers, Coach Wester turns to the bench and tells me to call "Motion to Win"—our kiss of death, our four corners, milk-the-clock offensive set to end games. The only shots that are to be taken are layups and free throws. Coach is losing his voice at this juncture, so *I can bark a little louder.*

But the facial expression on Stony Point's Head Coach, Antoine Thompson, goes from horribly bad to even worse as he recognizes the actions occurring simultaneously with the command, when Isaiah pulls his dribble back towards center court and the other East ballers move to the edge of the outer corners.

To close the game, we make 5/8 from the charity stripe, shooting 7/10—70%—in the fourth quarter, with Jordan 2/2, Narit 3/6, DJ and Xavier 1/2. To counter, the Tigers have zero free throw attempts.

After a timeout and with a minute remaining, Coach Wester takes a seat between Coach Godwin and me, and Godwin whispers, "You're gonna be a state champion, Coach." Before the words fully leave Godwin's lips, and not allowing himself to give one inch, Coach Wester springs out of his chair and yells, "Cross. Cross. Coach, call Cross." I walk to the midcourt line and vehemently bellow, *Cross,* with my hands gesturing the play call.

This is surreal. In the final seconds, jubilation is building on the bench. Everyone is standing with our arms raised and encouraging the largest basketball crowd we have played to—somewhere estimated around 8,800 in attendance—to join in, and they're reciprocating the excitement. It is deafeningly loud and overwhelming, but this is the dream coming to fruition.

The caption on the scoreboard: **Stony Point 41, Plano East 53,** is indescribable. Indicating that only four short years ago, East had come from the bottom of the district, and now we are here… the 6A Texas State Champs and with an improbable 40–0 record to boot.

I see myself falling back into my seat, like the scene captured in *Glory Road* when the buzzer goes off and the entire team rushes the floor in excitement. The assistant coach takes a second, grappling with his thoughts, and he accepts the reality that his team just did the unimaginable—winning the championship. But to the left of me is Xavier, and we have the best-ever, pressure-releasing bear hug of all time.

It is pandemonium all around the Alamodome. Coach Lambert, Coach Richardson, and nephew Jon have made it to the floor, as have Principals Jones, Eppler, Daniels, Lamar, Salazar, Flake, and Abdelfattah. Our Athletic Director, Jeff Smith, and Special Assistant, Sharon Rollins, and staff gather on the floor for the presentations as well.

I walk towards the stands where my family is sitting to receive my kiss and hug from my wife, Rebecca, and to bring the grandsons onto the court with me. Again, I want them to experience this moment too. I'm planting seeds for their future. Chauncey keeps them in tow.

Tears overflow everywhere. Not in defeat or because of sadness, but from joy and sacrifice, and from doubt to accomplishment. And tears not only from the players, but from parents, supporters, and the entire East Side of Plano. Out of this title run, seeds will be planted, dreams will be dreamt, and goals will be set.

I have my photo taken of me kissing the floor on the state championship logo—a bucket list memory, captured in the moment. A championship has been long overdue.

The celebration continues with UIL staffers handing out medals, first to the state finalist Stony Point players and coaching staff, lined up along the free throw lane. Coach Thompson is presented with the Runner-Up trophy, and a clapping ovation is granted and well-deserved.

Next, we line up at the opposite free throw lane for our medal reception and State Championship trophy presentation, which is handed to our Superintendent, Dr. Theresa Williams, then to our players.

After a couple more minutes, our entire group—cheerleaders, managers, trainers, players, and coaches—positions for the championship photo at center court. Seconds later, the players circle around the trophy for their rallying cry: *"Who's got my back? I've got your back!"* And when finished, they hustle over to the rather large East fandom, still in the arena, waiting for their acknowledgement of support. A tradition that started several years ago, the players thank the Eastside base with hugs and handshakes until the hostess signals for our assistance to leave the gym area and the fans to exit the dome.

There's no pace or jog this time to the locker room—only the slowest of slow, a meandering of steps is taken as every member absorbs this experience in real time. Upon entrance, you can hear the music blasting from the speaker and, when the door opens, lights are flashing from cell phones. Guys are dancing—dancing on tables, water being thrown, and towels waving, as they should. Partying like it's 1999, a Prince reference. Memories not long to be forgotten.

Somewhere during the locker room celebration, I can still remember the scene: Carter on the table, Chima dancing, as well as Ammani and the younger players. I begin to regret not getting those senior players into their final game as a Plano East Panther. Coach Wester always found ways to reward the fellas that sacrificed playing time during the week, and it's my responsibility to mention or keep him informed of such situations. With all the emotions and excitement clouding our minds in the last minutes, we missed the opportunity to clear the bench. The celebration is all the same, and no one cares who gets the credit.

The magic of magics has been accomplished. **40–0.** Perfect, undefeated State Championship in the biggest high school classification, 6A, in the state of Texas. **DONE.**

In summary, the state game is a microcosm of the 2023–2024 season for the Panthers. East dominates from the tip to the buzzer with a ferocious defensive effort. Stony Point led for 0:14 seconds. Biggest run: 9–0. Largest lead: 2 at 6:00 in the first quarter. East led for 30:24. Biggest run: 10–0. Largest lead: 12 at 1:24 in the fourth quarter. Game was tied for 1:22. Times tied: 2. Lead changes: 2 in the first quarter.

Round Rock Stony Point 41 – Plano East 53
RRSP: Josiah 18 pts, Hueitt 8 pts, Goodlet 8 pts
DJ 18 pts, 6 rbds; Rachard 13 pts; Jordan 8 pts, 8 rbds; Narit 7 pts, 5 rbds; Xavier 5 pts. But the unsung hero is our floor leader, Isaiah, who scores 0 pts, 5 defl, 7 stls, 2 asst, and takes 3 charges.
The Tournament MVP is none other than DJ, with a game-high 18 points.
Plano East 40–0.

A change of clothes into sweats and a quick once-over packing of the locker room, and to the Emily Morgan for pizza, more pictures, and celebration. While walking my wife to her hotel about 1 a.m., we unexpectedly find several of our players enjoying themselves on motor scooters around the Riverwalk. I encourage them to go to bed.

7:30 arrives early, but it's a great arrival. My wife and I take an early stroll about the Riverwalk and run into Jody Mazzola, our game announcer, and his lovely wife, on the sidewalk. We have a brief congratulatory conversation on last night's victory, and we continue to mosey up the *Paseo del Rio*.

Not soon afterward, as Rebecca and I approach the hotel, all of our players, trainers, and managers are coming from the basement breakfast area to prepare for our 10:00 checkout and the return to Plano. The Emily lobby is actively hopping with people checking in and out, others standing around sharing their experiences from the games or their weekend lodging in the heart of San Antonio.

Before the entourage boards the charter for home, we walk over to the Alamo and take a group photo with the state trophy in hand. There is a schedule to be kept. At the halfway point, the bus will stop at Buc-ee's outside Temple for snacks and shopping. The approximate arrival time to campus is around 4:00, per bus driver Mr. Ron. Coach Wester texts the coaches that an impromptu reception is in the making upon our return. This will be a surprise because the district and student body are out for spring break.

As the bus forwards past the four-way stop at Los Rios and Merriman, a line of cars can be seen turning into the staff parking lot. From the distance, an assemblage of Plano East supporters—give or take 200 or so—a couple news crews and reporters, are gathering outside the Archie McAfee Gymnasium. The accumulation to welcome home their 2023–2024 6A State Champions. A much bigger surprise than expected appears and exemplifies how hungry and appreciative the Eastside community has become. *A cherry atop the icing on a freshly baked cake,* I thought.

Bright and early, Monday morning, March 11th, after returning from San Antonio, Isaiah, Jordan, Narit, MVP DJ, accompany Coach Wester to the Fox 4 News studios to join Brandon Todd and the breakfast show. The first of spoils that come with winning a title. An appearance with the K104 radio show follows a week later. Several other public opportunities for the players to be recognized will come about in the next couple weeks, with the school board, the city council, feeder schools, and possible appearances with local businesses. Can it get any better than this?

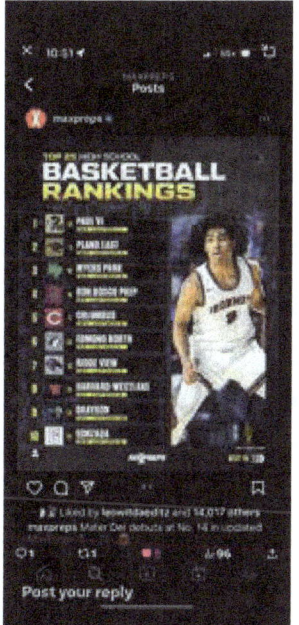

Regional Quarter Final

Round 3
79-52

PLANO EAST
2024
CHAMPIO

36-0

"Heros Come in All Shapes and Sizes"

Chapter XIV

EXTRA, EXTRA - The Throne

It can get better, and it is granted. With the success of the season, in state and nationally, the Panthers were followed and received an invitation to participate in a national tournament in New Jersey. *The Throne*, in its second year, is a highly prestigious high school national basketball tournament hosted by the NBPA and Gold Level Sports and Entertainment.

A partnership with former NBA/WNBA players is developing a high school March Madness event. A selection committee chooses the best 16 high school basketball teams in America to compete in New Jersey at the American Dream Mall on March 27–30.

Coach Wester had been in contact with a committee member since the CBI, but the interest in the tournament was on the back burner until our district competition was decided. With his full concentration on the state tournament, the opportunity resurfaced when answering emails on tournament dates. The interest and availability from the Throne representatives were requested, and Coach had to do his due diligence with our parents and students. He mentioned the Throne tournament and shared the information with our parents via email.

Before the regional tournament, the parents acknowledged that all of the players would be available if the final invitation was offered, and the invitation was revealed at halftime of the NBA All-Star Game.

Due to UIL Rules and Regulations, our players would play as a "club team" or "AAU team." The coaches could attend but would not have any coaching responsibilities. Former Plano East Assistant Coach Lambert would be coaching the team. The Panthers entered the tournament as the #2 ranked team in the nation, according to MaxPreps.

The plan was to fly out of Dallas–Fort Worth Airport on Tuesday morning, the 26th, and play a single elimination tournament beginning Friday, the 27th, at 11:30 a.m. against Homewood-Flossmoor, Illinois. If successful, they would play the winner of CHSAA/PSAL, New York vs. Oak Ridge, Florida, in the second round. Third round, Brotherhood, New Jersey vs. Bishop O'Connell, Virginia, and bracket championship winner, Richmond Judges, Virginia vs. The Vale, California.

Three weeks later, Coach Evans made the arrangements for the coaches to meet at Plano East for the Uber ride to DFW, while the parents did the same for their student-athletes, per UIL guidelines, and met for the 11:00 a.m. boarding. The plane landed at Newark Liberty International Airport at 3:45 (EST), and a shuttle bus delivered our team to the Hilton Meadowlands—Two Meadowlands Plaza, New Jersey—across the highway from the New York Giants practice facility and within five minutes from the American Dream Mall and MetLife Stadium.

Somewhere over the Tennessee or Virginia line, I was awakened by the plane as it shifted due to some rough air turbulence—from a dream, or was it the memories of September 11, 2001? That deadly morning the Twin Towers of the World Trade Center in New York City were attacked. A flood of images came rushing back of being in the library of Plano East, laminating posters for our student services program, and watching on the mounted television, Tower 1 burning with flames, then seeing a plane crash into Tower II, in real time.

The second tragic attack on our home front in the last five years—the first happening in Oklahoma City—was domestic, but the New York assault was foreign-based.

Just to think, the attacks occurred a couple of years before these young men were born. Their knowledge and understanding have come from documentaries, feature stories, and word of mouth. A few may have written a paper or possibly had group projects, but not one of them, I'm informed, had visited the site or been to Ground Zero. Hopefully, we could pay our respects to those lives taken that day, if time permitted.

The Throne Itinerary

March 26

6:00 – Welcome Dinner

6:30 – Meet and Greet – All Teams

7:00 – Financial Literacy: Chris Matthews, Danny Green, Kyle O'Quinn

8:30 – Event Concludes

After the opening ceremonies, following a four-hour flight and losing an hour, plus two hours of waiting in the airport, and no one wanting to admit it—today had been a long haul. Coach Evans and I, along with Coach Wester and Godwin, were roomed together.

10:00 p.m. – In your Rooms

12:00 a.m. – Lights Out

March 27 – Homewood-Flossmoor, Illinois vs. Plano East, Texas (First Round)

8:30 a.m. – Wake Up

10:15 – Depart for The American Dream Mall

11:30 – Tip Off

Two weeks of practicing against themselves, after school and away from the comforts of their surroundings, the Panthers returned to form with a strong defensive presence and spot-on shooting. East jumped out early and maintained a 20-point advantage over the All-Star squad representing the state of Illinois.

Behind Coach Lambert and Coach Coleman, East built a lead to 30 points much of the second half, with perimeter daggers raining from the multitude of teammates—Jon, Xavier, Isaiah, Narit, Ethan, Rachard, and DJ—each with two threes apiece, highlighted with Seth and Narit's first in-game dunks. Plano smothered Homewood.

Homewood-Flossmoor 65 – Plano East 90

Following the college-like celebration of putting the winning team's name on the bracket wall, we hung out in the mall and watched the girls' first-round game before returning to the Hilton for a late brunch.

Our next opponents, Florida vs. New York, scheduled at 6:00, gave the team four hours of free time to shower and rest. Coach Evans, Coach Godwin, and Coach Lambert had evening plans of visiting New York City well underway. We shuttled to the American Dream Mall for dinner—on your own—and met in the gym area before the game.

A good first period by both squads, but Florida took control of the match in the second quarter. Midway in the third, Florida was handily beating the New Yorkers when the decision was made to return to the Hilton before heading into the city.

The team Ubered into New York City. Four rides were called, and each of the drivers dropped us off in or around Penn Station off West 32nd, where the walk to Times Square began. It was a Wednesday night in New York, and the streets were jam-packed with people. *What a great experience and memory for the guys.*

We passed "Macy's" on West 34th/Seventh Ave, "The Shubert Theatre" on West 46th, and settled for pizza at Famous Famiglia Pizza off 8th Ave before heading back to Madison Square Garden, Chase Entrance "C" on West 33rd St, to return to the Meadowlands for the night. The sights and sounds of New York City were phenomenal.

12:00 – Lights Out

March 28 – Oak Ridge, Florida vs. Plano East, Texas (Second Round)

8:30 – Wake Up and Breakfast
12:00 – Depart for American Dream, Lunch, Shop

A few of the guys visited Nickelodeon Universe and the Water Park, relaxing their legs in the cold, indoor aquatic playground. Others perused the five-story build that houses 450 stores and is the second-largest mall in the United States. It features iconic shops, game rooms, a roller coaster, an ice rink (where the basketball games were being played), and fine dining.

2:00 – Return to Hilton Meadowlands, Rest
5:00 – Depart for American Dream
8:00 – Tip Off

The season came to an end after a hard-fought, overtime loss to a gamed Florida ball club. With the lead and ball in the final seconds of the game, we had a myriad of errors that sent the game to the extra period. Florida rode the momentum, making one more play than the Panthers—the philosophical strategy we've lived by all season—and pulled off the upset win. Our first and only defeat, **41–1**, was bittersweet but equally reminded us that it's part of the process.

Oak Ridge 78 – Plano East 76 (OT)

March 29

9:00 – Wake Up Call
10:30 – Team Meeting
Pack everything for home and bring bags to Coach Lambert's room.

12:30 – Meet in the Lobby, Uber to Central Park

5:00 – Depart for Newark Liberty International Airport

7:00 – Board for DFW Airport

The flights were booked for our return to the Metroplex, but we had approximately four hours before check-in. A group vote won by a landslide for walking around Central Park and sightseeing. It was a beautiful day to end a trip to New York. However, Chima and Moustafa overslept and caught up with the group an hour or so later.

In our group were Coach Wester, Narit, Jordan, and Ethan. We were dropped off at Central Park South and must have walked half of the 843 acres. I attempt to walk 10,000 steps a day, per doctor's recommendation, but today I was closer to 30,000. I treated myself to a street hot dog with sauerkraut and mustard, and a corndog with ketchup. *Not healthy, but it had to be done.*

On the shuttle, there was a little melancholy, knowing that this unbelievable ride to the best season in Plano East school history had come to an end—but not a soul was saddened. The goal was achieved, accomplished like no other. 40 wins and 0 defeats. This trip, although we were 1 and 1, was unexpected but well-deserved. And to visit the Meadowlands and New York City was the extra— the "Big Apple" of the bunch. So appreciative to be a part of such a historic season with this group of players and coaches.

No. 1 Plano East rolls over No. 10 Allen wit...

10:34

planoeastbasketball and
leowitdaeditz

PLANO EAST VS EATON
WHITE OUT
ROUND 4

MARCH 1, 2024
:00 PM AT WILKERSON-GREINES

Remind me

Liked by leowitdaeditz and 224 others

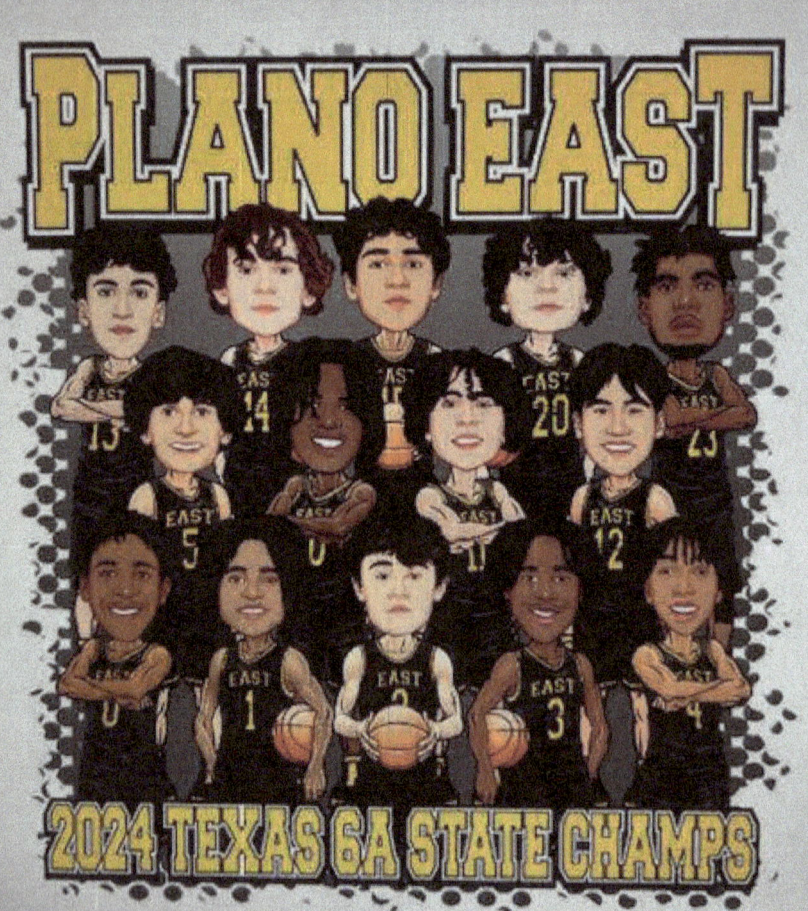

"Champions behave like Champions before they are champions. They have a winning standard of Performance before they are Winners."

- Bill Walsh

Chapter XV

By The Numbers

If the Texas high school basketball community knew that Plano East would be a force to be reckoned with, they were slow to acknowledge it. It began in June at the TABC Showcase, and everyone involved knew this team had everything they needed to compete for a state title.

We first traveled to Wichita Falls for the Elite 14 scrimmage against three of the best of Oklahoma. Then to Crowley to play in the Cowtown Tip-Off for the season opener vs. Allen High, an off/on district rival and known nemesis. This was followed with a trip to nearby Arkansas, before district play, against that state's best and the Oklahoma state champion, Owasso. East wins the "Hoopin' on the Hills Tournament" by 37 points over host Fayetteville High.

Three tournaments and three championships. All in all, this group has won seven tournaments in three years together. Coach Wester wanted to create the most challenging schedule possible and one that would prepare the Panthers for a rigorous district and playoff run.

Season:

- 31 games on the road.
- State-ranked teams: #1 Stony Point, #2 Stony Point, #8 Keller, #9 Allen, #10 Waxahachie, #11 Lake Ridge, #15 Mt. Pleasant, #17 Highland Park, Regional Finalist Rockwall, Area Champs Lake Highlands, Arlington Martin, Arkansas State Finalist Springdale High, Final Four Finalist North Little Rock.
- Regional Finalists: Leander Rouse, Keller High, V.R. Eaton.
- State Semifinalist: Mansfield Lake Ridge High.
- As well as four district teams ranked in the top 25: Flower Mound, Flower Mound Marcus High, Hebron, and Regional Semifinalist Lewisville High.
- 35 victories by 10 points.
- 29 victories by 15 points.
- 18 victories by 20 points.
- 17 victories by 25 points.
- 8 victories by 30 points.
- 5 victories by 40 points.
- 5 victories decided by 10 points or less.
- 13 teams scored 50 points or more.
- 1 team scored 70 points (Allen in the first game of the season).

- 3 teams scored above 60 points, but lost by 18, 21, and 27 points.
- 29 teams held to 10 points or less in a quarter.

(Playoffs)

- Bi-District: Rock Hill — 6 points.
- Area: Highland Park — 8, 9 points.
- Regional Quarterfinals: Allen — 8, 9 points.
- Regionals: Eaton — 8, 10, 2, 8 points; Keller — 9 points; Lake Ridge — 10, 9 points; Stony Point — 4 points.

The defense is the show. That commitment made all the difference. No one outside of the Panthers' locker room paid much attention to the Panthers' defensive effort until the scoreboard screamed the disparaging, double-digit leads at the end of a quarter. At intermission, it was briefly discussed, but eventually, they took notice when the final score lit up. Their defensive efforts were less than publicized in the media, but the defense became their calling card. It separated the pretenders from the contenders and shined the brightest when it counted the most—during the playoffs. The quote, "defense wins championships," is true.

Offensively, this is the most skilled team ever to wear the black and gold. They share the basketball; they cut and pass effectively and shoot the rock efficiently. Five members shoot over 40% from behind the arc. The team shoots 75% inside the paint area and 80% from the charity stripe. They score 0.75 points per possession and have a 1.2 effective scoring percentage.

The Panthers score above 70 points in 22 of 40 games, with a high of 95 against Flower Mound, and the lowest output on the year is 51 vs. Leander Rouse in the CBI tournament.

Historically great numbers for a team not nationally recognized as great individual players but a well-rounded, tightly knit collection of friends who love playing with and for one another.

Seasonal:

- 2,833 points = 70.8 ppg offense
- 1,924 points = 48.1 ppg defense
- +22.7 diff

Playoffs:

- 488 points = 69.7 ppg offense
- 324 points = 46.3 ppg defense
- +23.4 diff

All are school records. This group has rewritten both the offensive and defensive record books for team records but did not set any individual school records, except for going undefeated, 40–0.

"Think Positively and Masterfully, with Confidence and with Faith, Life becomes more Secure, more Fraught in its actions. Richer in its Achievements and it's Experiences."

-Eddie Rickenbacker

Chapter XVI

Awards and Recognitions

This team's sum is greater than its parts. Texas, over the past two decades, has developed some of the best high-end basketball talent, and the Dallas–Ft. Worth area has seen its share of future stars. Truth be told, 'it is a hot bed,' if I must say so myself. However, our East squad, unfortunately, is under the radar. Despite their skill set and success, coaches from the Power Five schools, Division I, or the mid-major level, didn't make the normal stop by Plano East like in the past. Only one player has a solid Division I offer.

Our players were made to feel underappreciated and, on most accounts, underrated, but we, as coaches, used their frustration with the process as motivation. We refocused on the big team goals of winning one game at a time and playing at my best this game, with the promise that the individual achievements would take care of themselves.

Coach Speaks tells the guys that there is no "I" in TEAM, and that is true. But there is an M and E. However, there is no team without the "Me's." The "Me's" must do his/her part to become a member of the team. When the "Me's" understand the work ethic, the sacrifices, the selflessness of everyone involved, the TEAM aspect becomes paramount. The I/Me ingratiates the group, and that's a beautiful combination.

They're a great group of basketball players.

Academic All-District:

Rachard Angton, Ethan Moss, Jordan Mizell, Seth Romero, Jon Tran, Narit Chotikavanic, Isaiah Brewington, Moustafa Abualneel

All-District:

6-6A Co-MVP: Jordan Mizell, DJ Hall

1st Team: Xavier Miller, Narit Chotikavanic, Jon Tran, Iasiah Brewington

2nd Team: Rachard Angton, Ethan Moss

All-Region I:

Jordan Mizell, DJ Hall

All-Region MVP:

DJ Hall

All-State:

DJ Hall

State Tournament:

MVP: DJ Hall

All-Tournament Team: Jordan Mizell

THSCA Super Elite Team:

DJ Hall (MVP), Jordan Mizell

AMAZN All-Star Game:

MVP: Narit Chotikavanic

Jon Tran, Ethan Moss

Maverick Tournament:

MVP: DJ Hall

All-Tournament Team: Isaiah Brewington, Xavier Miller

"Hoopin' on the Hill – Big Chicken Classic" Tournament:

MVP: Jordan Mizell

Whataburger "CBI" Tournament:

MVP: DJ Hall

All-Tournament: Narit Chotikavanic, Jordan Mizell

Head Coach Matt Wester:

40–0

6-6A Coach of the Year

Dallas Morning News Coach of the Year

Texas Association of Basketball Coaches Coach of the Year

Texas High School Coaches Association Coach of the Year

MaxPreps National High School Coach of the Year

Inside High School Sports, Title Belt

National High School Athletic Coaches Association Coach of the Year

Bobblehead Doll Recipient: DJ Hall, Matt Wester

UIL Assistant Coach of the Year:
Michael Godwin

UIL Middle School Coach of the Year:
Jaylon Simpson

5 Seniors Signed Basketball Letters of Intent:

- Xavier Miller – Bishop State, Troy, Mississippi Junior College, 2024. Transfers to Independence Community College, Division I JC, in Kansas, 2025.
- Narit Chotikavanic – West Texas A&M, Canyon, Texas, Division II, 2024. Transfers to Stephen F. Austin, Division I, in Texas, 2025.
- Jon Tran – Augusta State, Augusta, Georgia, Division II, 2024.
- Jordan Mizell – Tarleton State University, Stephenville, Texas, Division I, 2024.
- Amanni Koutsakis – Collin County College, Plano, Texas, Junior College, 2024.

- Chima Chineke – University of Iowa, Iowa City, Division I (football), 2024.
- DJ Hall – Texas State University, San Marcos, Texas, Division I, 2025.

Additional Recognition:
- The Throne High School National Championship Invite, East Rutherford, New Jersey.
- Recognized by the Mayor of Plano, Jon B. Muns, received a Proclamation from the City Council.
- Recognized by the Plano ISD School Board, by Dr. Theresa Williams, Superintendent.
- Recognized by Congressman Keith Self, U.S. Representative, 3rd District of Texas.
- Recognized by letter from Candy Noble, Texas State House of Representatives, District 89.
- Recognized by Nate White, Connect Dallas/UNT-Dallas/Senator Royce West, Texas State, 23rd District.
- Plano Juneteenth Celebration Parade (The team was Flag Carrier).
- Dick's Sporting Goods (Allen) Poster Signing and Photos.
- The Backyard (Murphy).
- Sweet Firefly (Richardson).
- Archie McAfee Gymnasium, Poster Signing and Photos.

Attitude is a Choice,

-Pat Summitt

Chapter XVII

Epilogue

The general perception by outside coaches is that this group of players, friends, are overachievers, and nothing could be further from the truth. They are the most skilled group of players to ever suit up for basketball at Plano East. They are a strong-willed bunch of ballers.

At least three or four times between 2008 and 2016, our Panthers had enough talent to make a serious run for a state 5A title – not could have, but should have – and didn't. Believe me, there have been many conversations at the local barbershop on the subject. It's inexplicable how things work for the will of God. Most times He says NO, and for good reasons. February 24, 2023, was an emphatic NO answer. None the wiser, that night was preparing this group for something really, really special.

Other times, He says SLOW, again for reasons beyond our understanding. For five years in a row, we failed to qualify for the extra season, the playoffs, including the 2017–2018 season when we didn't win a district contest, going 0–14. Some long drives home and sleepless nights ensued.

So many things could have occurred in those games to change our outcomes during that stretch of seasons. Situations we had control over, and a few not so much. On occasion, I still blame myself to this date with a couple of those misfortunes. Wisdom and perseverance prevailed; all things work for the good of those called according to His purpose.

Then there are times He says GO, and everything just works.

2023–2024 was the GO year. We had a fine-tuned machine of players, an exceptional group of coaches, and a philosophy that allowed all the moving parts to pull in the same direction.

Twenty years have passed since Coach Adair walked me into Principal McAfee's office with the request for me to join his staff as an assistant coach. I remember that day as if it were yesterday. Eager to prove myself on and off the court, Coach gave me my first assignment before we entered the gym locker room: "Take So-and-So into the office, call his father, and tell them both that there WILL NOT be a repeat of last season's antics. If there's any ripple of the water, he is gone… and so are you!"

Not an up-and-under move. Not a block-out drill. A parent call. An ultimatum for both of us. A great relationship with the player and family came because of that phone call.

'I was excited about helping the team to a return trip to the playoffs, possibly a district championship after a four-year absence, but my thoughts at that moment were, I may not make it through the tryouts.' We accomplished all three goals in that first season together. Eighteen months later, Coach Adair passed away.

In pursuance of 20 years since this quest began, Plano East boys' basketball hadn't sniffed a trip to the Alamodome in San Antonio to play for the title.

March 9, 2024, we took ownership: "Started from the bottom, now we here."

I had the best view in the building. Not a front-row seat but THE catbird seat, first chair! I'm not the man, but I am next to the man with a master plan. It was the epitome of awesomeness, the holy grail of Texas high school basketball: the 6A Boys State Championship Title Game.

At night's end, my Plano East Panthers had sought and completed the first 40–0 undefeated, perfect season in Texas basketball's highest classification, 6A, and the first undefeated champion since Duncanville in 2007.

By the way, on May 13, 2024, UIL proposed a new basketball format. There will no longer be regional tournaments and no more Final Four gatherings. The governing body voted to split all the divisions into big school and small school, resembling football, which changed the format two decades ago in 1990.

On June 11, 2024, the UIL committee approved the proposal to restructure the postseason for volleyball, basketball, softball, baseball, and soccer. There will now be two state champions per division.

The 2023–2024 Plano East Boys Basketball team will forever be recognized as the last undisputed, undefeated 6A State Champions in the highest classification of Texas high school basketball history.

'Some people are Destined to be brilliant for an incredible amount of time and others are Destined for just a moment.'

Chapter XVIII

Reflections

Through these lenses, give or take some 20 years plus, I've witnessed 11 playoff appearances and 8 district championships, all similar yet dissimilarly constructed; even if they mirrored foundationally, their makeup is independently appreciated.

Personal reflections should remind all that this is only a game and there are so many other things of more importance like family, health, or our fellow human beings, but that's not my lot in life.

I so much looked forward to competing in a kid's game twice a week that it compels and dictates my summer, winter, and spring vacations—or it has since my daughter, Quinae, picked up the game of basketball in her 7th-grade year.

Today, with and through these young men's ever-changing eyelids, is my passion and, be damned, is the bane of existence. It is one of the most rewarding adventures a coach and players can immerse themselves into with no guarantees or promises, only bonds and memories—some good and others not so good, but memories all the same.

I'm not a believer, nor have I entertained the coach-speak, "Enjoy the Process," and all that it entails… but I now have a better understanding of this philosophical point of view.

After a week away from campus due to district-wide spring break, which falls on championship weekend every year, I asked the players and coaches to share their engaging perspectives or memories of this magical and historical basketball season. These are the responses to questions on their journey throughout our 2023–2024 basketball season and on capturing the 6A State Championship.

Amanni, Sr:

1. What was your biggest obstacle or worst experience?
My biggest obstacle was NOT letting my playing time affect my mood and enjoyment.

2. What were your thoughts on the new lighting and player introduction?
I thought that the fog lighting was so cool, and it really got the crowd involved.

3. What was the scene or feeling at the Alamo?
It was amazing, it felt like a March Madness game.

4. What was your favorite playoff moment?
The dog pile.

5. If you could change anything about your high school basketball journey, what would it be?

Nothing, it was a perfect season.

Seth, Sr:

1. Describe your favorite basketball experience in 2024.

   Playing in the Throne National Tournament because it was a new and rare opportunity.

2. Explain your thoughts on playing Stony Point in the CBI tournament.

   Going into the game, I was confident and excited but nervous because at that point, it was the most attention East had gotten in a single game, and it was the #1 vs #2 team in the state.

3. What was your favorite team moment?

   After the game, walking around downtown San Antonio as a team. It was the most rewarding experience.

4. Discuss your best basketball accomplishment.

   My best basketball moment was being able to prove myself as a player worth being put in the rotation during close games.

5. Describe the scene at the Alamodome.

   Looking out into the stands before the championship game, seeing thousands of filled seats was such a gratifying thing. It felt good getting recognized on such a big stage.

Chima, Sr:

1. Explain what your biggest sacrifice would be becoming a member of the team.

   Accepting my role as someone who would not play much but be supportive and cheerful of my teammates.

2. Tell your favorite coach's memory or experience.

   When we were taking pressure free throws and Coach Wester was smiling because he knew I would miss it, but he called my name anyway. I missed the free throw, and he laughed, and we ran.

3. Share your thoughts on playing at Plano East and in the Jungle.

   Playing for East means a lot to me. I really like the community and everyone around it supporting us throughout our season. It's a surreal experience and anyone is lucky to be a part of it.

4. Who was your least favorite opponent to play?

   Plano Senior, because up until my senior year, we never beat them at all, not even in football. But it was good to finally get the better of them.

5. Describe your biggest basketball fear coming into 2023–2024.

   My biggest overall fear was underachieving, given how good and talented our team was. We knew we could make it to state, and that goal became clearer as the season progressed.

6. What was your motivation?

   To simply win. Whatever I had to do, I wanted to win. If it was playing 0 or 30 minutes, I just wanted to win and finish on top.

Ethan, Sr:

1. What was your biggest obstacle or worst basketball experience?

   One of my biggest obstacles during the 2024 season was not knowing how many minutes I was going to get each game due to our team having so much depth, but still preparing and focusing in every game in case my name was called to step up.

2. What was your favorite gym to play in?

   The Curtis Culwell Center, playoff game against Allen. It was a sellout and the loudest gym I've ever played in. I got my first college offer after the game.

3. Tell your favorite coach's experience or funny memory.

   When Coach Thomas had to use the restroom so bad on an away game that he made us pull the bus over and stop at a McDonald's. We ended up using the women's room because the men's was full in use.

4. Describe the emotions in the locker room before the championship game.

   It was the most locked-in we've been as a team. Although in most games we were always joking and playing around, which is just how we operated as a team, that championship game brought out a different level of focus from everyone.

5. What was your motivation?

   My motivation to win state wasn't necessarily for myself, but for all of us as a team and as friends. Growing up with these guys and seeing how hard they all work pushed me to work even harder for them, knowing how badly we all wanted to win state for each other.

6. What was your biggest basketball accomplishment?

   Getting named to the 2nd Team All-District. I definitely wasn't expecting this award, but it felt good to see my hard work be acknowledged.

Moustafa, Jr:

1. What was your biggest obstacle?

   Being a sophomore and not getting as much playing time due to having so much depth and senior teammates.

2. Tell your favorite coach's experience or funny moment.

   Hanging out and riding to the Arkansas tournament with Coach Smith.

3. Explain the ice baths.

   The ice baths were very hard and uncomfortable, but the environment with the teammates was all worth it.

4. Describe your favorite basketball experience in 2024.

   Winning the Arkansas and State Championship, going 40–0.

5. What was your favorite team moment?

   Riding the electric scooters with Jon and Izan around downtown San Antonio after winning the state championship game.

DJ, Jr:

1. What was your biggest basketball accomplishment?

   Being named the MVP of the state tournament.

2. What was your memory from the Arkansas tournament?

   Winning the championship by 40 points.

3. What was your favorite playoff moment?

   Scoring 30 points against Keller in the regional finals and knowing that we were going to the state tournament.

4. What was your motivation?

   To prove to all my doubters who said I wouldn't be anything!

5. If you could change anything about your high school journey, what would it be?

I would invent a time machine so I could go back and relive this season.

6. What was your worst basketball experience or obstacle?
Overcoming injuries my sophomore season.

Isaiah, Sr:

1. What was your worst basketball experience or obstacle?
Injuries. I never had to experience injuries until this season. Breaking my nose and a severe thigh contusion was detrimental to my health and was a motivation to keep playing. I didn't care about the healing process, I was eager to get back on the court and help my team win.

2. Explain your biggest sacrifice to becoming a member of this team.
My biggest sacrifice would be scoring points. I had to play the leadership role of getting the ball to my teammates rather than being the man to score.

3. Most memorable moment from the Arkansas trip?
For me, it was meeting Coach Nolan Richardson, the legendary Razorback basketball coach.

4. What was your favorite team moment?
The team coming to my house to support me after my nose was broken.

5. Describe the scene at the Alamodome.
The dome was much different than a real gym. The court

was bigger, the rims were smaller, the fans were louder, the lights were brighter, and the eyes were all on us.

6. What was your motivation?

My motivation was to do it for the city that never let me down. Do it for the people who always supported me. Do it for Jesus Christ who put me in this position. Do it for the brothers who I've seen bleed, sweat, and cry over the season. Do it for the memories and say WOW, we went 40–0.

Xavier, Sr:

1. What was your biggest sacrifice of becoming a member of this team?

My sacrifice was playing my role and not worrying about who was shooting the ball, while learning to become a better defensive player.

2. What was your favorite playoff moment?

Playing against Allen in my childhood city in front of all my family and friends.

3. Describe the Alamodome scene.

The dome felt like we had all the eyes on us. From the jump, when we walked into the arena until we walked out. It built us up.

4. What was your motivation?

My teammates were my motivation. Trying to do it for the

person beside me and to win it for him, because I knew they did the same.

5. Explain your thoughts on the ice baths.

   Personally, I only took the ice bath on Thursdays because ice baths are not for the weak, but we made it fun and enjoyable. We always had good laughs and developed a bond. It's memories we'll remember forever.

6. What was your favorite basketball experience in 2023–2024?

   Going to New Jersey for the Throne National Tournament.

Narit, Sr:

1. What was your biggest sacrifice to becoming a member of this team?

   Not playing football and choosing to go all in on basketball.

2. What was your worst basketball experience or obstacle?

   Always being doubted. I used the doubt as fuel to prove everyone that I can play, to prove them wrong.

3. What was your least favorite trial or situation while on the basketball team?

   Coming off the bench—but it was for the betterment of the team.

4. What was your favorite team moment?

   All the road trips and winning the state championship.

5. Describe the emotions in the locker room before the championship game.

It was the best locker room type atmosphere I have ever been in. Not a lot of talking, everyone was zoned in because we knew we were going to make history.

6. What was your favorite coach's memory?

Seeing the pure excitement and joy of all the coaches as soon as the buzzer went off.

Jon, Sr:

1. What were your thoughts on the new lighting and player introduction?

It was one of the most indescribable and surreal feelings I've ever felt. I remember testing it out with Coach Thomas during the daytime and thinking it was the stupidest thing. The lights were tiny, handheld, and not very bright. But when it happened, it blew me away. I remember being the last of the starters to be introduced, and with the whole crowd screaming your name, it was unique and I felt like I was going into battle with my brothers.

2. What was your favorite team moment?

Besides all the fun we had as a team, one of my favorite memories was a serious one. Hours before the championship game, I was with Jordan and we were thinking about how this was the last game we were going to play together. As a core, we began in the 7th grade, but a smaller group like me and Carter, or the GBD1 guys, it was more like the 2nd and 3rd grade. I called everyone to our room, and we talked about the game plan, best case scenario, worst case outcome, etc. Once we were done, someone had the idea of telling our favorite memory of the season. We all stood in a circle, and it was very emotional. Some guys, including myself, started tearing up. It was cool to see how thankful everyone was for the season.

3. What was your motivation?

   Fighting for something that was so much bigger than myself. On the toughest days, when we had to run tons of sprints during pressure free throws because no one was making their shots, I thought about what we could accomplish. The pain, the struggle, and doing it for each other, our school, and what we'd dreamed about for so long pushed us through every day.

4. Explain your sacrifice to becoming a member of this team.

   The sacrifice many of us made being on this team was taking a lesser role for the benefit of the team goals. Any one of our core guys could've been the man at a neighboring school—taking all the shots, attention, and running the team at a lesser program. But we knew we wanted to do something nobody had ever done before, and we wanted to do it together. I knew I wouldn't get as many shots as I did my junior year, but I was okay with that as I began to really understand the chance we had to win the state championship.

5. Discuss your best basketball accomplishment.

   It was with the future panthers and kids in general that I, and us as a team, inspired. The attention we gained brought young fans from everywhere to come witness what was happening. Getting to sign autographs for young kids after the playoff games was one of the coolest experiences ever.

Jordan, Sr:

1. What was your worst basketball experience or obstacle?

   Getting injured my freshman year against Rowlett.

2. Explain your thoughts on playing Stony Point in the CBI Tournament.

   It was good to get that hard competition in early and to know we had the ability to focus and beat a team like them. It prepared us for a deep playoff run and gave us a confidence boost entering district.

3. What was your expectation for the 2023–2024 season?

   I was most excited about how we finished last season giving the state champions, Lake Highlands, a run for their money. We were bringing back almost our entire team for a chance to win state.

4. What are the team's best assets?

Our team chemistry. We know each other from way back. It's like we think on one brain. We know the backdoor cuts, the pop-out threes, and teams can't keep up.

5. What was a teammate's favorite moment?

Ethan's dunk against Flower Mound.

Rachard, Sr:

1. What was your motivation?

I was excited to get back on the court. It was a little over a year of recovery from an ACL injury I suffered before the beginning of my junior season.

2. What's one of your biggest obstacles on the floor?

As a shorter player, I maximize my strengths: shooting and speed. Even though I am small, I play some of the best defense and I'm most energized when I enter the game.

3. Explain your thoughts on the ice baths.

We are built for this. Tough!

4. What was your feeling on Senior Night?

There were a lot of nerves, but those nerves go away when you get into the game and remember all of the work you've put in. It was cool to see all the fans and family coming out to support. It was the first time people began to pack the stands.

5. What was one of your favorite basketball experiences?

    The Oklahoma team camp and staying on campus.

Carter, Sr:

1. Describe your favorite basketball experience of 2024.

    To do what we did was amazing. We never thought this could happen. We all grew up together, had dreams, and stuff—but possibly making history or being one of the best teams to ever play in Texas wasn't the talk. We just liked doing stuff together. To see how far we've come and to make dreams a reality, it's crazy and amazing.

2. What was your favorite playoff moment?

    Hanging out with my childhood friends and teammates.

3. Discuss your best basketball accomplishment.

    Getting a tough bucket in the Throne Tournament against the Illinois State Champs.

4. Share your thoughts on making it to state.

    We had to grind. Nothing was given to us. Every hangout we had starting in the sixth grade led up to the state championship. The summer workouts, sleepovers, bike rides—we were one huge family.

5. If you could change anything about your high school basketball journey, what would it be?

    Nothing. I wouldn't have done it any other way. I had the best high school experience I could have asked for, and it's

all because I got to spend it with a group of brothers. I
absolutely love every single one of them.

Izan, Sr:

1. What was your favorite playoff moment?
   The only thing I was thinking about was running onto the
   court and celebrating with my teammates.
2. Share your thoughts on making it to state.
   It was a surreal experience.

Managers

KJ, Sr:

1. What was it like to be a part of and witness the season?
   I wasn't with them my junior year, so seeing this for the
   first time was an all-around great experience. I was so
   grateful for the opportunity to see them prosper and grow
   as a team. It was awesome—I loved it and it was a great
   experience.

Kaylee, Sr:

1. What was it like to be a part of and witness the season?
   It was a really cool experience to see them go this far. I will
   never forget this season. I'm proud of them.

Gabby, Sr:

1. What was it like to be a part of and witness the season?
   I was here from the beginning of August, since tryouts, and to see how they grew and made it to state without losing a single game was crazy.

Coach Evans:

1. Describe your favorite basketball experience in 2024.
   By no surprise to me, it was the experience at the Final Four in the Alamodome. I started going to the state tournament when I was in 8th grade, back in 1984. That Christmas I asked my parents if we could get tickets to the championship at the Drum in Austin. That year started a tradition that went strong for 20 years with my dad. When I started coaching, I dreamed of being part of a team that played at the Final Four and realized quickly it was no easy task. To finally live that dream with a team I coached was incredible, to say the least.

2. What was your favorite playoff moment?
   Beating Allen High at the Garland Curtis Culwell Center. As an Allen graduate who once played there, facing them in the playoffs with our perfect season on the line was an exciting experience. The crowd was huge, the intensity was high— and we hammered them.

3. Describe the emotions in the locker room before the championship game vs. Stony Point.

I was amazed at how focused our guys were. When Coach Wester spoke and then Coach Thomas spoke, they were locked in like I had never seen before. They knew what was at stake and it was obvious they wanted this championship and to finish 40–0.

4. What was your motivation?

For me, it was just doing my part—showing up early, staying late, and doing all the things a good assistant should do. I had no idea the season would turn into the most incredible professional experience of my career.

Coach Smith:

1. What was your most memorable moment from the Arkansas trip?

Bonding with the guys, hearing them constantly crack jokes on each other—and on me too. Even the ride back playing freeze-out.

2. What were your thoughts on the new lighting (fog lights) and player introductions?

I thought it was cool for the guys to get an NBA-type feel.

3. What was your favorite teammate moment?

Watching Narit come in each game and give the spark

when it was needed. His drive and passion on the court each night were truly inspiring.

4. Share your thoughts on making it to state in San Antonio.

   It was awesome to see how a great group of guys who put TEAM over SELF came to work day in and day out, no matter how monotonous. They worked, worked, and worked. They had a goal and went after it.

5. Describe the emotions in the locker room before the championship game vs. Stony Point.

   The guys were completely locked in. You knew it was the moment, and they knew it. It wasn't the typical locker room we see from East players—they meant business. It was a special day for a special group of young men.

Coach Godwin:

1. What was your favorite teammate moment?

   One of the best was when Xavier threw down a huge dunk against Lewisville at our place. The gym was packed, and it was a close game. That play sealed the win and the crowd went crazy.

2. What were your favorite playoff moments?

   The game at Curtis Culwell Center against Allen, in front of the biggest basketball crowd that arena has ever seen. The environment will always stick with me, and the East fans gave us energy all night. And of course, the championship game—the drive, the locker room, warmups, the game, the ending, the celebration. One of the best experiences of my career.

3. Describe the scene at the Alamodome.

   It was breathtaking. A scene and a place I'd always dreamed of being part of, as a player or coach.

4. What was your motivation?

   To give everything to this group of guys. They worked so hard from when they were kids to middle school to now. I wanted to give them all my energy and time. They deserved success.

5. What are your thoughts on making it to state in San Antonio?

   It's such an accomplishment to be one of four teams in Texas to make the tournament, and then one of two to play for a championship. There are so many great players, teams, and coaches in this state, which makes it even more impressive.

Coach Wester

1. Explain your thoughts on playing Stony Point in the CBI Tournament.

   When we faced them the previous June in the TABC Showcase, it became clear that we would be two of the three or four best teams in the state. The players and coaches checked their scores and stats all season long. We knew they had the highest-rated player in the state, Josiah. Going into that game, we knew it was likely a preview of the state championship. I remember telling the players in the locker room that this was technically a meaningless game—just a measuring stick—but we wanted to win it. More than anything, I reminded them: If we wanted to be the best in the state, we needed to beat them in March.

2. What was your favorite teammate moment?

This team was so close. The way they cared for each other, loved each other, and enjoyed each other is what made them special. After practice, they would just hang out in the locker room. They never wanted to leave. They could've gone to someone's house, but they loved Plano East and what they had built. From the coach's office, we could never tell what they were doing—we just knew they were having fun because they were laughing so hard. Eventually, I'd blast honky-tonk music loudly through the locker room, and that's when they'd finally leave.

3. What was your most memorable moment of the Arkansas trip?

The highlight of the trip to Fayetteville was getting to meet Nolan Richardson. He's one of the greatest coaches in the history of the game. It was an honor to shake his hand and talk about life, basketball, and family with such a great man. He told me, "I almost never leave my home. I haven't been away from my wife in a year. But I am coming to these games because of this man right here." He pointed to Coach Greg Thomas and added, "I've only been to two or three games in the last decade, and I'm excited to be here and see you guys play. This is the guy who would get me in the gym again." He sat behind our bench for two games. It was intimidating to have a Hall of Fame coach sitting behind you while you coached—I was mortified I might say something wrong. But as always, the guys played their hearts out and once again made me proud.

4. What's your favorite coaches' moment?

It's hard to pick just one. Winning a state championship is so incredibly hard that nobody will ever understand the adversity you must endure to build the resilience to win it all. When the season finally ended, the celebration was amazing, but for me, I couldn't enjoy the time on the floor as much as I wanted. There were press obligations, pictures, award ceremonies, and a good bit of chaos. When we finally got back to the locker room, it was 11:30 p.m. The coaches had our own dressing room within the locker room. After we changed into our suits, we all came together, hugged, and took a photo. That moment was the culmination of so much hard work and sacrifice. We were 40–0. Several of the assistant coaches are well qualified to go on and be excellent head coaches, and we didn't know if we would ever be together again in that capacity. We love each other so much and are grateful for the experience. That photo, taken by Coach Chris Foley—our trainer who started at Plano East the same week I did 12 years ago—is the most memorable photo of my career.

5. What team traditions meant the most to you? *We started a tradition of having the team over at my house for a Christmas party, and then again after the last regular season game before the playoffs. I think it's good for my wife and five children to see that when I'm away from home, I'm doing work that matters and making a difference in kids' lives. I also want the players to see the sacrifices coaches make to be with them. I made 85 smash burgers on the griddle for them—they devoured them all. When finished, they fired up the fire pit, grabbed some blankets, and made themselves at home. They stayed on the back deck and played video games for the next two hours. My children and the players had a blast. That's what I miss most about this team: hearing them laugh together and enjoy one another.*

Do not let what you cannot do INTERFERE with what you can do!

-Coach John Wooden

Chapter XIX

Quotes/Books

Quotes & Inspirations

"You cannot live a perfect day without doing something for someone who will never be able to repay you." – John Wooden

"At the end of the day, nobody cares about the box score, only about the result."

"It's not the will to win that matters—everyone has that. It is the will to prepare to win that matters." – Paul "Bear" Bryant

"Hard Work, Expectations, Attitude, Recovery, Toughness."

"The best thing you can do for a person is to inspire them. That's the best currency you can offer." – Nipsey Hussle

"Self-discipline begins with the mastery of your thoughts. If you don't control what you think, you can't control what you do." – Napoleon Hill

"Winning is not a sometime thing; it's an all-the-time thing. You don't win once in a while, you don't do things right once in a while, you do them right all the time. Winning is a habit. Unfortunately, so is losing." – Vince Lombardi

"You can't cheat the grind. It knows how much you invested. It won't give you anything you haven't worked for."

"Most people have the will to win. Few have the will to prepare to win." – Bobby Knight

"It's all in the journey. The process is only valued when hard work delivers."

"Everyone must choose one of two pains: the pain of discipline or the pain of regret." – Jim Rohn

"Always remember that leadership is a privilege. When you are in a leadership role, your influence may affect the trajectory of people's entire careers—and often, their lives."

"The bond that links your true family is not one of blood but of respect and joy in each other." – Richard Bach

"Consistency wins. It's what you do every day that counts." – @bechampionminded

"Heroes come in all shapes and sizes."

"Champions behave like champions before they are champions. They have a winning standard of performance before they are winners." – Bill Walsh

"Think positive and masterfully, with confidence and with faith. Life becomes more secure, richer in its achievements and in its experiences." – Eddie Rickenbacker

"Attitude is a choice." – Pat Summitt

"Some people are destined to be brilliant for an incredible amount of time, and others are destined for just one moment."

"Do not let what you cannot do interfere with what you can do." – John Wooden

Influential Books

- *How to Lead When You're Not in Charge* – Clay Scroggins
- *War of the Worlds* – Alfred Hitchcock
- *Strengths-Based Leadership* – Tom Rath
- *They Call Me Coach* – John Wooden
- *Teammates Matter* – Alan Williams
- *Legacy* – James Kerr
- *A Season on the Brink* – John Feinstein
- *Mighty, Mighty Matadors* – Al Pickett
- *Got to Do Some Coachin'* – Frank Deford

- *Made in America* – Sam Walton
- *The Winner Within* – Pat Riley
- *The Book of Basketball* – Bill Simmons
- *Coaching Basketball Scramble Defense* – Jim Larrañaga
- *Offensive and Defensive Drills for Winning Basketball* – Lyle Brown

Acknowledgements

In my home office sits an old wooden desk built by my wife's grandfather, a computer, a bucket of pencils and pens, and a large dry erase board. To the right is a leather couch from Rebecca's 8th grade classroom, with books stacked as a makeshift shelf. The floor is covered with chapters of this manuscript, some used, some misplaced, but always accessible if needed.

On the recliner, in clear view, rests the beautiful picture of the team circled up around the free throw line—chosen as the front cover of this book. On the back cover is the photo of the five coaches—Godwin, me, Evans, Smith, and Wester—taken in the locker room after the state championship game. Both will be submitted as covers for *#MakingBelievers*.

I wish to thank, directly or indirectly, all who were involved and who followed our program on this historic journey of 2023–2024: the many columnists, journalists, sportscasters, and coaches for your input, styles, and coverage.

Thank you – Craig Smith, Matt Welch, Matt Diggs (East Alums), Paul Miranda, Kenny Matthews (*Friday Night Glory*), Robert Hatter, Jim Hicks (*The Chop Shop*), Kyle Grondin, Randy Jenning, Brad Harris, Lisa Assimakopoulos, Myah Taylor, Greg Riddle, DeDe and the Morning Crew (especially J. Kruz), Brandon Todd (*Fox 4 News Good Day*), Pat Doney (*NBC 5 Inside High School Sports*), ABC 8's Joe Trahan, *Murphy Monitor*, Texas UIL Sports, Plano ISD, Plano East Administration, Plano East Athletic Staff, Trainers Solis and Foley, PESH Prints, Photographer Roosevelt Joubert, Photographer/Videographer Leonard Ratliff.

It has been my pleasure to serve as a coach at Plano East during such a special time. I was blessed to be part of a staff alongside an extraordinary group of young men who faced challenges of hard work, perseverance, disappointments, setbacks, and sacrifices—and pooled it all together to capture the biggest prize in Texas High School basketball: a state title. To cap it off, they went 40–0 in 6A, the largest classification in Texas, in the most dominant statistical fashion to date.

About the Author

Greg Thomas is the award-winning author of *No Doubting Thomas: Hawg Whisperer – My Arkansas Memoirs,* a five-time recognized book chronicling his four-year journey as the first Black starting quarterback at the University of Arkansas. During his tenure as a Razorback, the program appeared in four consecutive bowls and amassed a 35–13 record.

#MakingBelievers is his second nonfiction book, with the trilogy *9th & Randolph* currently in development.

Greg is entering his 29th year with Plano Independent School District in the Student, Family, and Social Service Department, and his 22nd as a varsity assistant basketball coach at Plano East Senior High.

He and his wife, Rebecca, have a blended family of seven children and eight grandchildren. They reside in Celina, Texas.